Managing More with Less

Managing More with Less

Joanna Howard

OXFORD BOSTON JOHANNESBURG MELBOURNE NEW DELHI SINGAPORE

Butterworth-Heinemann
Linacre House, Jordan Hill, Oxford OX2 8DP
225 Wildwood Avenue, Woburn, MA 01801-2041
A division of Reed Educational and Professional Publishing Ltd

◈ A member of the Reed Elsevier plc group

First published 1998

British Library Cataloguing in Publication Data
A catalogue record for this book is available from the British Library

Library of Congress Cataloguing in Publication Data
A catalogue record for this book is available from the British Library

ISBN 0 7506 3698 X

Composition by Genesis Typesetting, Laser Quay, Rochester, Kent
Printed and bound in Great Britain

Contents

Acknowledgements

I have always worked like a jackdaw, collecting bright and interesting ideas. Not much in this book is original, only perhaps the way of putting it together. In the text of the book I have acknowledged the authors I have collected from. I have acknowledged under changed names, for reasons of privacy, some of the many people I have met and learned from, by telling their stories in the book. I want to take the opportunity here to acknowledge the less visible contributors. First, Loretta and Jean my assistants who have patiently typed, amended and printed (on a very slow printer) draft after draft. They have also paid me the compliment of reading it and commenting on the parts that they themselves found useful. The fact that they read the draft as well as typed it helped me to write in "normal" language rather than management jargon which I easily slip into.

Long before the typing began, in fact years before, my colleagues at Roffey Park often exhorted me to "write some of this down", paying no attention to my slothful excuses that "it was meant to be ephemeral". I want to thank in this respect particularly Sheila Evans, Judith Martin, Nick Jeffery and Andrew Constable. They will probably recognise some of their ideas blended into mine. The people with whom I co-trained in those days shaped or challenged my thinking in various degrees – noticeably Jackie Keeley, Andy Hunter, Jenny McKeown, Paul Roberts and David Lines. Ian Cunningham had an empowering influence on my thinking, while I was still at Thames Polytechnic. I have been part of a learning set for some time now, who have helped me clarify my ideas: thanks for that and for robust support to Christina Evans,

Eden Charles, David Lines and Paul Ballman. Linda Holbeche of Roffey Park gave me the opportunity to do the book. It has been a great experience doing it, and I am grateful to Linda for the chance to "get it down in writing".

I have always had the problem that after hearing or reading an interesting idea, as soon as I begin to use it I believe I thought of it myself. Apologies to anyone whose ideas or help I have not mentioned here and should have.

Among the most influential people in my life, certainly the ones who taught me the most, have been my children (and their father) and grandchildren, who continue to impress and delight me. A final thank you and acknowledgement to them.

Introduction: More of what? Less of what?

This book is designed to provide possibilities and food for thought for people who wish to be genuinely effective in their use of time, energy, resources and spirit; balancing the competing priorities they experience at work and in the wider landscapes of their lives. Many of us are being asked, or are asking ourselves, to manage or deliver more results with less resources. I am including in this book ways of managing more than results, and looking at other items which we may have or want less of.

Many of the people who I have worked with describe their experience as one of managing:

- more complex and interdependent issues
- more people reporting to them
- more stakeholders with an interest in the results of what they do
- more responsibility
- more demands on their time
- more expectations
- more pressure for results

and they would prefer to have any of the following:

- less effort
- less misdirected energy

- less stress
- less wasted time
- less cost to themselves
- less cost to others
- less malaise and dissatisfaction
- less frustration.

The whole understanding of what it is to manage at work is changing, from an ordered, moderately predictable hierarchical role to one that is more like conducting an orchestra (sometimes without the score). Within this role we work with increasingly scarce resources and often need to give increasingly demanding jobs to employees or colleagues who are already under pressure, some of whom do not work in a direct reporting line. Strategic goals inevitably shift, and so do success criteria. Different stakeholders may become more demanding. We are asked to respond to demands for increased productivity, increased effectiveness, better parenting, increased customer or user satisfaction and, in the case of the profit-based sector, increased return to shareholders and return on investment.

As well as this, people at work are increasingly trying to balance their time at work with child care or elder care, and even to have some time or energy for their own development and personal life. More and more people are not in paid work, and are having to manage with less certainty, less traditional job satisfaction and, often, less money.

When we look at the wider picture, we are beginning to realise that the environment is not as abundant as we had been assuming. It is becoming clear to us that mineral resources are finite; there are fewer fish in the seas, the wide biological variety is being reduced as species become eradicated; the ozone layer is being diminished. Although a large proportion of the world's population enjoys a standard of living higher than that of their parents, an astonishing proportion live with malnutrition and in extreme poverty. This is illogical considering the amount of food and other resources available in the world. We are trapped in an economic system that leads, inevitably as it seems, to more people having to manage with less in the interests of other groups having more.

As we get to know more about this, we may wish to manage more effectively and more sustainably in the wider context, with a realistic approach to our long-term future. This may mean escaping from a way of thinking that puts economic growth and individual wealth at the forefront of national and individual priorities. The accustomed separation in thinking and behaviour between our life at work and our "normal life" begins to seem untenable, not a realistic possibility. The costs are having to be borne somewhere, generally by someone else; at a personal level by our own families or our own health and in the wider context in pollution, burnout, unemployment or unethically low wages.

It makes sense to think more widely about what we are doing, and review the assumptions underlying what we do and how we do it. Set in this kind of framework, managing more with less makes sense. We could genuinely use less resources, energy, time, for a greater gain, instead of getting our results for the same price but making sure that someone else pays.

It may be surprising to read about these issues in a book about new management skills. An ability to position oneself in the wider context of one's whole life and of the world, however, is part of the emerging portfolio of skills required of the manager, whether managing in an organisation or managing one's life.

The topics I discuss in the book are drawn from my experience as a manager, a teacher, a mother and a consultant working in a wide variety of organisations and countries. I have realised that managers are by no means the only people who "manage", and I have learned a great deal through watching and working with all kinds of people managing complex situations, with reduced available resources, in a way that satisfies them and other stakeholders, in very many different settings.

The skills and approaches that I have seen people use and have used myself fall into nine overlapping categories, some or all of which they use much of the time:

- They think strategically and creatively, even about short-term activities, and they know how to manage their thinking.

- They use project management as a way of thinking as well as a way of managing projects and intuitively use "backwards planning" as an approach to critical path thinking. They believe in streamlining things and getting them to flow. "Firefighting" does not attract them, even though they are well able to act effectively in an emergency.
- They prioritise intelligently, realistically and proactively; with a wide focus where appropriate. This helps them to stay cool under pressure. It also helps them respond to the inevitable disappointments and losses that are part of living.
- They are skilled at influencing without authority. They connect with others' priorities to help themselves and the overall direction of the organisation or group they are working in. They are true delegators and are able to let things go completely when appropriate.
- They value and understand difference because they know something about themselves, and also about other people, and the kind of combinations that help them to manage more with less. They do not waste time or energy in criticising or objecting to difference, even when they truly disagree. They just get on with things, building on or working round the differences.
- They have a realistic understanding of their relation to time and of how they "manage time". They distinguish between really urgent (life and death situations) and things that seem urgent. They have a philosophical picture of their life as a whole as well as the moment they are living in. They know that time means different things to different people, and can work with that.
- They look after themselves, seeing themselves as their own greatest asset. They are able to notice when they are not working to their best, and they do something about it. They look after their emotional and spiritual development as well as their professional and work-related development. They have a great ability to have fun.
- They are great learners. As well as this, they get ready for the next part of their life by living this one well, really knowing how to live in the present.
- They have an interactive viewpoint, seeing themselves as part of a bigger system. Because of this, chaotic or complex situations do not unnerve them unduly, because this is how they understand life anyway.

Using the book

The book works with two levels of thinking. I see it as important to discuss our immediate level of experience, "I have too much to do – more responsibilities, more demands, higher expectations – and less time and resources to do it with", and to look at ways of improving the situation in terms of ways of thinking and behaving. Sometimes it is valuable to look also at the deeper level, reviewing and sometimes challenging the assumptions that underlie the pressures that many people experience. These assumptions operate both personally and organisationally, and are also discussed in the book.

Each chapter contains a variety of discussion, activities and examples. It is not written to be read through at a single sitting. It is probably useful to skim through, to get an impression of how it is structured and the overall picture, and then choose the parts that appeal to you. My aim is to provide a map, with some routes, a landscape of approaches to the business of managing in complex and demanding settings, which can be used by each reader in their own way.

One of the problems I see with management books is the tendency to offer the "new improved formula" that we are all looking for. Please do not use the book like this. Nothing in here is new; it is only a bringing together of what ordinary people do, when they give themselves the chance to think for themselves and check out what actually makes sense for them. See this book as an opportunity to give yourself that chance.

1 Thinking skills – unclutter your thinking

Introduction

● One of the problems many of us give ourselves when we have a heavy workload or are managing conflicting priorities is that we do not take time to think, or to think about our thinking.

● As well as this, a situation which is complex or chaotic (in the sense that many different things are happening which do not seem to be predictable or manageable) can be so challenging to our thinking that we either revert to old simplistic patterns or feel paralysed and helpless. It is often tempting to look for a recipe for success; a theory or framework into which we can squeeze reality. Managers and people in business are especially prone to this.

● In these and other ways we may inadvertently choose ineffective ways of thinking, rather than ways that increase our general capability. Many managers say they "do not have time to think". In fact, thinking well takes no more time than thinking badly or just worrying. Much of our thinking can have the effect of "clutter": getting in the way, making it hard to find what you want, difficult to sort out. This chapter will be looking at different ways in which you might streamline your thinking, and make it more appropriate to the work in hand.

● The topics that are dealt with move from the more personal types of thinking, to thinking in a wider context. They include how you think when things go wrong, or you think that they may go wrong; the flexibility of your thinking; your style of thinking in complex or ambiguous situations; and your ability to think strategically.

Using this chapter

The chapter is not designed to be read right through. It brings together different approaches, by which you can first review your thinking and then, if appropriate, attune and align it, so as to manage pressures or challenges in an economical way that works for you and the people around you. The Roman philosopher Epictetus said that people are not disturbed by events themselves, but by the view they take of them. This chapter will help you to be more aware of the view you are taking of things, and the way you think about difficult or pressuring work issues.

You can use the activities in the chapter to develop alternative views and a way of thinking that will bring you to the position where you can be more effective without putting yourself under more pressure. It is probably most useful to skim through and try a few of the activities using a live situation of your own, then later on come back and try a few more. Taking the opportunity to try different ways of thinking can be refreshing and energising. And at least one of the activities, probably more and possibly unexpectedly, will be of real value to you.

"The manager's most vital responsibility is to manage the thinking efforts of the organisation, in such a way as to ensure that it makes the best decisions about its future . . ."

The type of thinking that a manager is responsible for is different from, though certainly no less important than, other uses of human thought, such as philosophical, aesthetic, scientific or mathematical thinking (from *The Professional Decision Making* by Ben Heirs, 1987)

An effective thinker should know which kind of thinking is needed at a given time, and is able to do it or participate in it (from *Effective Decision Making* by John Adair, 1988)

Becoming aware of how you are thinking

Here are two activities to start with:

1.1 Becoming aware of how you are thinking

Step 1   *Choose something difficult you have to do in the near future.*

Step 2   *Think about it in your normal way.*

Step 3   *Notice and describe your way of thinking about this challenge. This may mean standing outside yourself as if you were observing your own brain and the way you think about this topic. Notice whether there is a particular conversation going on internally. What would a person hear, if they could hear your thoughts, as you think about a problem?*

Step 4   *Notice any emotions connected with your thinking, emotions such as enthusiasm, anxiety, satisfaction, complacency, antagonism to others.*

Result   *This activity gives you the opportunity to notice how you are thinking. It can also be the basis of a very effective habit, that of checking "How am I thinking about this?" particularly in a difficult situation or where you have a dilemma to be resolved or a choice to be made.*

1.2 Thinking differently; transferring ways of thinking

This activity gives you the opportunity to enter into other ways of thinking by imagining yourself engaged in a different type of activity. The challenge is to find out to what extent you can increase the flexibility of your thinking about something that is currently facing you and to transfer approaches from one situation to another.

Step 1   *Choose a task or situation that you are currently dealing with or getting ready for. Reflect on it and review your plans briefly.*

Step 2   *Now set that aside and choose one of the three situations below. Imagine you are:*

- *at the helm of a 60ft. racing yacht*
- *a bridge builder*
- *a skilful surfer . . .*

What kind of thinking would you be doing in the situation you have chosen? What would be the important things to be thinking about?

Step 3   *Going back to the original situation in your own life that you thought of in Step 1, find something in these ideas that would transfer in a general way, and that would enrich your ways of thinking and dealing with it:*

- *Think about your job as if you were a gardener: consider how a gardener thinks about a garden. What are the particular things they pay attention to? If you were thinking about your job in this way, what would you be doing and how would you be thinking differently? What might you be paying attention to that you are currently ignoring?*
- *Warrior thinking. What would you be thinking about if you were involved with war, with fighting, with protecting the innocent. If the task or topic you are considering was to be described in this way, how would your priorities be affected?*

○ *If you were hosting many welcome guests to a great event next week, what would be going through your mind? If you were to think about your job in the same way, what difference would it make?*

Result   *As you do this activity, you may notice particular qualities in your thinking, some that are flexible and some that may seem a bit stuck or rigid. You may also find some new ways of viewing your current work.*

When Frances, an independent consultant, used this approach, she found that each of the metaphors helped her to add something to her thinking. She had a fairly active consultancy, and was taking some time to reflect on how she might develop her business. She was also a keen gardener, so using this metaphor was easy. This was in August, and she was planning to buy bulbs to plant in September, choosing different bulbs to flower successively from January onwards. She was also wondering how to get the garden to look better next August, as its best time seemed to be June. Transferring this to her business development thinking, she realised that she needed to plan more activities that would lead to work next year, and look for a mixture of long-term and short-term work. At the moment she took few initiatives herself as she got most of her work by responding to immediate requests. Nor did she picture how she wanted her consultancy to look next year, as she automatically did about her garden, and she saw this as a way of thinking that could usefully be transferred.

The "warrior thinking" did not appeal to her straight away, but she had a go at it. How would she be thinking if she were a compassionate warrior? She imagined that she would think about keeping herself fit and well trained to use her weapons; she would think about maintaining her supplies, about studying the enemy, about placing those she was protecting in places of safety, well defended and well provisioned. Transferring these ways of thinking to her business thinking, she found it surprisingly useful. The idea of keeping herself fit and skilled in using her weapons reminded her to plan in some training or development for herself in the coming year, and to find time to follow up her plans for a co-mentoring relationship with an ex-colleague. The idea of studying the enemy transferred in two ways. She decided to pay more attention to "the enemy within" – her own habits which reduced her effectiveness, which at the time included a reluctance to see herself as a professional business and untidy ways of working with paper. And trying to consider "the enemy without" triggered the realisation (even though they were not her enemies) that she needed to study the overall businesses of her clients and their competitors more carefully.

Surfacing your own assumptions

When I was part of a research group looking at the characteristics of effective leaders of creative groups, Phil Salmon, an educational psychologist, introduced us to an activity she had devised which helps people notice how they are framing their understanding of a particular situation; what kind of assumptions they are making. "I call it the Salmon line," she said, "not just out of immodesty, but because it seeks to draw forth something lively from below the waterline. Being essentially a line – no more than a line – it is infinitely flexible."

The activity involves using a line to represent some kind of progression: for example, a scale of competence, steps towards a goal, easy to difficult, profitable to unprofitable, likeable to unlikeable. The participants mark points along the line which represent noticeable differences along the continuum. They need to be specific, giving examples of what each point signifies. They then look at what is required to move up or down the line.

The process is easier to understand if it is seen in practice. Here is an example of the way I used the activity, following Phil Salmon's model, with a group of managers. They drew a line which represented a continuum of employees who were "easy to manage", at one end, to "difficult to manage" at the other end. They then wrote in along the line the initials of particular employees for whom they were responsible, in terms of how they experienced them as easy or difficult to manage. They were asked to put a note beside each set of initials to explain why they had located that person at that point: what were the characteristics that gave them that particular place on the line between easy and difficult.

They then talked to each other about the lines they had drawn, and were asked to discuss the *characteristics* that located an employee at a particular place on the line. (They were discouraged from discussing the employees themselves.) The managers found that being "easy" versus "difficult" to manage meant very different things to different people. As well as this, it became clear that being "difficult to manage" is not the simple opposite of being "easy to manage". The phrases which people had written to describe employees at either end of the line were by no means the opposite of each other.

I then asked the managers to think about the employees they had been describing, in terms of what it would take for any one of them to move along the line. What would need to be happening for the employee who seemed difficult to manage to become easier to manage, in the eyes of the manager doing this activity? How far along the line could that employee reach if things went really well? What would enable that to happen? Conversely, if those who were now easy to manage became difficult, what would be the typical change and how far might they go towards the other end of the line? What would be the critical circumstances that might lead to that happening?

Again the managers were asked to discuss with each other what they had done and what they were discovering. It was interesting and rather surprising to explore "what it would take" for an employee to move up or down the line.

The managers found out a great deal about their own assumptions and mind-sets about management and motiva-tion. They became much more able to distinguish between what in the discussion and in their original thoughts was about themselves, and what was to do with the employee.

Moments in the process of thinking: de Bono's six hats

As well as looking at one's own assumptions and typical ways of thinking, it's useful to widen our sense of our options in styles of thinking. Edward de Bono has a well-known way of encouraging people to use a variety of thinking styles. He describes six different ways of thinking, calling them "six thinking hats". The six ways of thinking he describes are in the areas of emotions; perceived difficulties; perceived possibilities; creative alternatives; facts and figures; and planning and boundary-setting.

Acknowledging the emotions involved

The emotions involved in the way we address a situation affect the way we view it, and have a strong effect on how we select and value different evidence. Acknowledging in an objective way the emotions we are experiencing in a situation helps us to be aware of how this might be operating. It also has an energising and liberating effect. Seen as a normal part of the thinking routine, people can understand that acknowledging the feelings involved gives us another set of useful data.

At the same time it is important not to value emotions differentially. In some families or organisations, some emotions (such as enthusiasm) are highly valued and described as "positive", and other emotions (such as grief, or even fear and reluctance), are dismissed as "negative". In the context of managing complex priorities, and in looking at how we are thinking, all emotions need to be acknowledged as current facts, neither positive or negative. In fact, the entrenched optimism, "commitment" and enthusiasm which are often favoured in organisations can lead to as many failures of business or relationships as can a more "pessimistic" approach which at least is aware of possible problems. The importance in using this kind of thinking is to be aware of the emotions involved, seeing them all as valid, and including the nature of the emotions involved as useful information to be included in how we think about a situation.

Looking for difficulties

The faculty of critical assessment, of being aware in an objective way of the problematic areas of a situation, leads to a particular kind of thinking. This thinking can be used to look for gaps, and for seeking relevant information. It is the style used when looking back on previous experience of how things can go wrong. It is not a "negative" approach unless it is the only one used; its strength lies in looking for difficulties that need resolving.

Looking for possibilities

The ability to think about the positive aspects of a situation builds well on the critical assessment and problem-aware approach. This way of thinking leads to constructive suggestions, a commitment to effectiveness and making things happen. During this kind of moment in our thinking we can develop a vision of how things could be, and how this could be put into effect, with a sense of the value and benefit of this course of action. It can be seen as a bias towards the *possibilities* rather than the problems or difficulties, and is another valuable aspect of thinking, although not on its own.

Looking for alternative solutions

Given the emotions, the problems and the possibilities, creative thinking about *alternative solutions* becomes possible, going beyond the obvious or even the possible. This kind of thinking requires the willingness to turn things upside down, to start from the other end, to build on ideas in a creative way, generating new and unexpected possibilities. It is a style of thinking that needs to be free of judgements, free of reasons why "it couldn't work" – that can be kept for a later phase. This style, or this moment in the process, is the hardest to do when under pressure or when feeling stressed.

Seeking facts and figures to be clear about the relevant data

"What are the facts? What do we know, what information do we need?" The frame of mind that seeks facts and figures, not in order to prove or disprove a case, but in order to be clear about the data and information available is an essential aspect of thinking. This moment calls for questions such as how many, how often, in what circumstances, which outcomes. It can be difficult to move into the neutral frame of mind that is required to make the most of this aspect, because so often we are required to use "facts" to defend a position, or to take an adversarial approach. Western culture with its folklore of "Lies, damn lies and statistics" and the selective use of scientific and statistical information in political situations has not equipped us well to be neutral information-seekers. Information is probably never value-free: our reasons for seeking it and the mental framework in which we acquire it and make sense of it mean that for each individual the information will be something different. Nevertheless, the effort to move into a moment of thinking in this way, freed of the emotional implications, can have a calming effect. This can be true even in situations where the facts are themselves horrific. The calming effect is partly due to our ability to use the facts to develop a strategy.

Mapping and planning

In order to develop a strategy, a sixth form of thinking is called for, in which we take an overview of the problem, reflect on the kind of thinking required, articulate and clarify the questions to be asked. This is a disciplined kind of thinking that has an element of control both over the thinking required and the way other people fit into the plan. In this moment of thinking you have moved on from argument, and a sense of purpose and an overall "map" of the situation is developed.

You may like to reflect on which particular style of thinking from among those described by de Bono you are more likely to engage in, and which ones you typically omit; and to find a way to widen your repertoire to include all six.

1.3

Step 1   *Think of a current tough situation challenging you such as shortage of resources or a deadline that is too tight.*

Step 2   *Divide a sheet of paper into six sections, heading them with six different aspects of the thinking that needs to be engaged in:*

- *acknowledging emotions*
- *assessing problems and past experience*
- *assessing possibilities and constructive actions*
- *generating alternatives and creative ideas*
- *collecting neutral information*
- *mapping the whole situation, taking an overview and making plans.*

Step 3   *Write down your thoughts as you consider the situation in each way, writing the appropriate thinking into each box.*

Step 4   *Review the effect this has on you.*

Table 1.1   Six ways of thinking
What is the situation or problem? It is about how to . . . or whether to . . . ?

What are my emotions in this?	What are the difficulties and risks I can see in the situation?
What are the possibilities and constructive opportunities?	What creative alternatives can I generate?
What are the basics of factual information I have?	What is my overall purpose and what needs to be done?

Words and language and their relationship to thinking

As well as noticing and developing your ways of thinking, making them fluid and effective, it is essential to notice your use of language. Almost everyone has a particular kind of language that they use when thinking and talking at work. Take a moment to reflect on the kind of words you yourself are inclined to use when you think or speak about activities, plans or deadlines when you are under pressure. You may find that you have used simplistic patterns that are not helpful and may even be dysfunctional in that situation.

Sometimes the language comes out of or reflects certain thought patterns; conversely, sometimes language that is used sloppily, as an old habit, triggers self-defeating thought patterns that do not help you to deal effectively with the current situation.

This particularly includes language and thought patterns which demonstrate wishful thinking, excessive feelings of obligation, unchallenged "life-rules" or "drivers", or blaming attitudes.

1.4 Wishful thinking language

Step 1   *Find an instance when you might be inclined to use words or concepts summed up by "if only . . .". For instance,*

- ○   *"if only I had more time . . ."*
- ○   *"if only people would listen to me . . ."*
- ○   *"if only I weren't so tired . . ."*
- ○   *"if only my colleagues would take more responsibility . . .".*

Step 2   *Pick one that represents a real wish; something that would really make things easier.*

Step 3   *Then transform the "If only . . ." sentence into one which starts with "Given that . . ." and continues with "What's my plan?"*

For example, you can transform the "If only I had more time . . ." example into "Given that I feel I don't have enough time, what's my plan?" (The answers could include "Stay harassed" or "Organise my time differently" or "Cut down the things I do" or "Prioritise differently".)

Generally the "plan" needs to include one of the following:

- ○ *"I'll put up with things the way they are"*
- ○ *"I'll do something to change the situation" (specifying what you will do)*
- ○ *"I'll shift the way I feel so that the 'if only' doesn't bother me so much"*
- ○ *"The first step I'll take to improve things is . . .".*

Step 4 *Go back to the "if only . . ." phrase and write down specifically what you would do, if "if only" wishes were granted. For example, for the wish "If only I had more time . . ." consider how exactly you would use more time if it was given to you. What specifically would you do, and what would the benefits be. If the wish "If only people would listen to me . . ." were granted, what would the person wishing it say to the people involved?*

Result *You will find that something in your thinking shifts, and you feel less trapped and more able to improve the situation.*

1.5 Obligations language

People sometimes use language which implies that they or other people are totally obliged to do things:

- ○ *"I've **got** to get this done in time"*
- ○ *"I **mustn't** let her down", or*
- ○ *"we **mustn't** let the share price fall", or even*
- ○ *"we must retain our market share".*

Although it's fairly normal in an everyday sense, it can be problematic when already under pressure or dealing with competing priorities.

Step 1 *Write down a few phrases that describe things you feel you **must** do.*

Step 2 *Check for the background of these obligations; which may include things you were taught as a child, concern for others, fears for job security, assumptions about the economic situation; while remembering that but few of our "musts" reflect a law of the Universe.*

Step 3 *For "must" or "got to", you substitute "I want" or "I choose to". Notice what happens to the sentence itself and its meaning for you; and notice how you react. If it seems clear that you do not in fact want or choose to do the things you feel you "must do", you need to explore further where the sense of "must" is coming from.*

Result *This small shift in language (often strongly resisted by people) can liberate a lot of energy and relieve stress. It can also move you from a feeling of being powerless and at the mercy of other people's needs or rules, to a more empowered position where you know what your choices are and why you are making them.*

1.6 Life-rules language

Step 1 *Read the next two paragraphs*

Sometimes people's thinking is coloured by a set of rules or assumptions that have a stronger than necessary effect on their thinking. They link in various ways to ways of thinking about obligations. Most people have an an almost unconscious assumption about how they "must" or "ought to" be. Some of us are striving to be perfect and have an excessive fear of failing; others believe they must always be strong, never showing weakness; others of us are driven by an unchallenged rule that we must be unfailingly pleasing to the people we are in contact with, and fear disapproval or dislike; many of us were brought up to try hard all the time, putting ourselves and others under untoward pressure; or to complete things quickly, never be late, work fast.

It is important to look at the drivers behind the way that you think about your work. There may be some overly powerful life-rules that are leading you to be inappropriately hard on yourself or others, in the way you think and the way you act. These life-rules almost always link to fears: fears of what would happen if you did not follow the rule implicitly.

Step 2   *Notice to what extent you believe you **always** have to or ought to*

- *be perfect*
- *be strong*
- *try hard*
- *be in a hurry, or*
- *be pleasing to other people,*

and notice to what extent you use this kind of language to yourself.

Step 3   *If one of these assumptions does act as a driver, you may find it helpful to, almost playfully, make a case for the opposite. Let us hear it then for not being perfect, not being strong, not trying, being lazy, etc. How could you describe the "opposite" in attractive rather than unattractive words?*

Step 4   *You may also wish to explore what you subconsciously think might happen if you did not follow the life-rule that you are particularly affected by. What would actually happen if you were weak, did not try hard, were not perfect, etc?*

Result   *You may find a freeing effect, or a feeling of surprise that you have been working from assumptions that are stronger than you realised; and that may no longer be valid.*

Stephen, an air traffic controller, was doing a responsible and demanding job. His father had been in the army and had brought him up to be reliable, effective and to have a strong sense of duty. When he tried this activity, he noticed that he was working to a powerful rule

"I must always be strong."

He realised that this inclination was of great use to him in many situations, and made him a valued colleague and friend, especially in times of crisis. There were other situations, however, when it was extremely problematic. His daughter had been very ill, and although she leaned on his strength, she told him later that she had not been at all sure that he minded or had any sympathy for her, because his way of showing his strength included not showing his emotions. Even his colleagues, he guessed, would have warmed to him more had he showed some uncertainty or vulnerability from time to time. It was quite a struggle to find values in the opposite of strength, or "weakness" as he described it, because in the way he was thinking about it, it was unmanly, pathetic and rather revolting. After a while he came up with some ideas. "People who are not always strong, can show their emotions when it matters, and other people may value that. Pretending to be strong when you don't feel it is false, too, and I wouldn't want to be false. Too much strength can leave you muscle-bound or rigid" – and at this he began to smile – "like some old boxer . . . that's not for me. I want to have a more, well a more supple strength, that knows when to let go."

Margaret, a systems analyst, when she tried this activity, found that she was particularly driven by a wish to be perfect, to get everything right. In her own mind, the opposite of "be perfect" was "be imperfect or flawed". Reluctantly she tried to make the case for *not* being perfect. "People who *aren't* perfect are . . .". The words came slowly, then more and more freely "easier to be with; human; forgivable; able to learn; flexible, etc., etc.". Doing this didn't change her from wanting to do things as well as possible; it did make her able to be more selective about when to aim high, and when "good enough" was more than good enough. In this way she actually became more effective, and was also less hard on herself and others.

1.7 Blaming language

Another clue to the way you are thinking is the language you use, internally or externally, when things go wrong. If you are inclined to say "Who's to blame?", or "It wasn't my fault", rather than "What went wrong?", it could be that you are not thinking clearly enough about goals and targets, and sensible strategies.

Step 1   *Think of a situation where you were or are inclined to blame yourself or someone else.*

Step 2   *Review the situation in a different light. Instead of asking "Who was to blame?", or blaming yourself, ask the questions "What exactly went wrong?", "How did it come about?", "What was the person blamed genuinely trying to do?", "What was their positive intention?"*

Step 3   *Reflect on to what extent this gives you useful solutions to the situation.*

Step 4   *Notice to what extent you are attached to the need to blame. How easy do you find it to let go of the blame? In what way does the activity of blaming deflect your energy from changing the situation?*

Result   *Seeing that there are other ways of thinking than blaming when things go wrong can give you the freedom to use a more effective strategy, and to look for ways of prevention.*

1.8 Metaphors

The metaphors we use ("grow or die", "bring out the big guns", "walking on thin ice") demonstrate and reinforce how we are thinking about our situation. Changing the metaphor can shift our thinking.

Step 1 *Notice which metaphors you are inclined to use in the ordinary course of conversation.*

Step 2 *Try a different set that reflect your own experience in a different way, or more appropriately. If you are stuck for ideas, try drawing on contexts such as sailing, building construction, air-sea rescue for your metaphors.*

Summary *The language traps described above may reduce your effectiveness, partly because they do not describe your situation accurately enough in the present, and partly because they relate to previous experience which may not be relevant now. Once you have escaped the traps, or reduced their effect on you by becoming more precise and specific, even in your use of metaphors, your thinking is released to become more creative, more strategic and a more fitting tool to help you manage the complexities of your work.*

Rational emotive and cognitive approaches

From the day you are born till you ride in the hearse,
There's nothing so bad that it couldn't be worse.

Albert Ellis, the founder of "rational emotive" theory, and Aaron Beck who described his approach as "cognitive" looked at the way people thought about difficult things, and the internal conversations they had, in response to what they saw as threats or difficult situations. Ellis assumed that individuals are naturally able to think rationally, but tend to slip into the habit of taking on irrational beliefs. When we are using language such as "It would be terrible if . . ." "It would be the end of the world if . . .", "It would be disastrous if . . ." in everyday work situations, we are speaking as if nothing could be worse than the feared event happening. We do not really mean this, and we know it; and yet we persist in using this exaggerated language. Ellis suggests that at the moment we use it, we do indeed think that nothing could be worse. This is a way of thinking that does not match reality, and may lead us to behaviour that is not rational and, in fact, works against us.

Ellis suggests that we should work with non-dogmatic preferences, rather than "musts". This means that we consider the tough things that may be going to happen, and describe what we want in terms of preferences rather than in terms of "I must have it", or "It must not happen". This allows us to deal with the possibility of the opposite happening in a realistic way, and this in turn helps us to work proactively rather than in a way that is driven by fear.

A person may be unconsciously working from a strong but vague assumption:

"I *must* please my boss whatever happens."

This might make them overanxious and focused primarily on pleasing the boss rather on than doing a good job for its own sake. Paradoxically, this may lead them into behaviour that reduces their effectiveness and, as a result, in fact displeases their boss.

A first step in improving this situation might mean expanding the thought into a "non-dogmatic" preference (leaving out the word "must") using accurate and specific language. For example,

"I *prefer* to please my boss because . . . (for example "it will make my job easier and more secure").

The next step needs to follow logically (for example in this case, "I had therefore better find out what pleases her").

And at the same time, a further logical step can be taken: "I can learn to cope with the displeasure of my boss if need be."

This kind of thinking does two things: it deals sensibly with the "must" feeling so that at least the person is working realistically with it. It also frees them from being driven by the assumption; by the time they have examined the assumption, as in the example just given, they find that they stop and think in a more effective way about the way they relate to their boss in general (in the example given) and what they actually want to do. This leads to behaviour that is chosen and realistic, and which achieves the original goal more effectively.

Ellis also suggests that we should work from a basis of self-acceptance thinking. This means accepting ourselves for what we are, including our potential for making mistakes. This makes it easier to learn and progress, by learning not to make the errors again. People who allow themselves to think of "failure" as catastrophic are much less able to pick themselves up and move forward.

Hope

Hope is the emotion or tendency that helps us react in a particular way to what might be seen as defeat or failure. A psychologist studying students with different levels of hope (C. R. Snyder, quoted in Goleman, 1996) suggested that hope was a better predictor of academic success than the conventional aptitude tests administered at the start of their course. He commented "students with high hope set themselves higher goals and know how to work hard and attain them". This is not the "hope for the best" kind of hope but rather an attitude of expecting the best and working for it, even in difficult or disagreeable situations. It also means a kind of resilience that does not easily give way to overwhelming anxiety, and does not take one defeat as a prediction of future defeats. Martin Seligman (1992) in his book *Learned Optimism* suggests that optimism and hope are ways of seeing events, so that good events are seen as normal, connected to oneself and long-lasting, and bad events are seen as limited, external and temporary. Pessimists or people without hope would see things in the opposite way. He suggests exercises for "training optimism".

It may be useful to reflect on your own experience: do you naturally expect things to turn out well or badly? How do you react when they do turn out well or badly?

The basic skills of strategic thinking: managing complexity

There are two kinds of people in the world – those that think there are two kinds of people in the world and those that don't.

Thinking "left brain" – "right brain" and getting the balance

Wherever it is that it may happen in the brain neurologically, our thinking can be seen as balancing into two complementary approaches - each of which supports and enhances the other. It can be tempting to value one kind over the other. Table 1.2 gives a picture of the two aspects suggested by the phrases "left brain" and "right brain". When dealing with multiple priorities and a complex workload, it is particularly important to get the best from both approaches.

By integrating these two styles and linking logical thinking with intuitive thinking, we can take a real strategic approach. This means being able to think in steps, sequentially, but also synchronously. It means breaking down tasks or activities into chunks whilst at the same time carrying a picture of the

Table 1.2 "Right brain" and "left brain" thinking

"Left brain"	"Right brain"
Logical	Intuitive
Step-by-step thinking	"At-the-same-time" thinking
Looks for structures, categories	Looks for patterns, flows
Explains by cause and effect	Explains by synchronicity, fuzzy logic
Directional, future oriented	Contextual, present oriented
Uses words, numbers	Uses images, puns, metaphors
Analytical, reductionist	Integrative, holistic

whole. Words and numbers are used effectively whilst also picking up or conveying meaning by images, puns and appropriate metaphors. Structures are set up that respond to flows. Cause and effect ideas do not exclude noticing and working with patterns and coincidence. In this integrated way of thinking the value of individual effort is understood, but in the context of collective responsibility and interdependence. Responding to "hunches" runs alongside looking for and incorporating data into the decision-making process.

The ability to integrate different perspectives, possibilities and ways of thinking while maintaining and reviewing a sense of overall purpose is the basis of strategic thinking.

1.9 Combining "left brain" and "right brain" thinking

Step 1   *Look through Table 1.2. Where do you think your thinking and problem-solving preferences lie – primarily as "left brain" or as "right brain".*

Step 2   *Choose a small decision that you are dealing with at the moment. Notice what your style has been in dealing with it. See whether using both approaches enriches your way of thinking about it.*

Result   *Integrating "right" and "left" brain approaches can sometimes give you a sudden insight – a new wisdom in viewing a situation and coping with it.*

Thinking in chaotic or complex situations

Chaotic in this context does not mean completely disorderly. It means the kind of situation where a chain of cause and effect is not apparent. It means a situation where small changes or individual actions have unexpectedly large and unpredictable consequences, and interconnectedness within the system rather than functional separation. And it means that although there are few obvious chains of cause and effect, there are patterns visible, a "family resemblance" or mirroring that can be recognised; and what happens in a small part of the organisation may resemble or represent what is happening more generally in the organisation or even more widely.

People who succeed in situations of this nature tend to be able to think about what they are learning, to be less concerned with cause and effect than with "seeing how things turn out"; being ready to adapt to unpredictable outcomes. Their thinking is concerned with looking for patterns, with developing new mental models, and with attempting to understand the whole interconnected system as well as the separate parts. They tend to look for analogies rather than reasons – "what is this like?", "what does this remind me of?" rather than "what caused this?" – in order to make plans or to understand what is going on. They make plans to manage the discomfort of transition rather than attempting to avoid, pathologise or deny the discomfort. They think as realistically as possible about what *is* happening, rather than what "ought" to be happening. They do think about the future, but in terms of describing a desired future state that is wide-ranging, rather than making cast-iron plans, and they continually adapt their thinking to new realities.

Ralph Stacey (1992) suggests that we shift our frame of reference in various ways. Acknowledging conflict, testing assertions and engaging in public dialogue is more to be valued, he suggests, than developing cohesive groups operating in a state of consensus.

Decision-making, in Stacey's view, needs to be seen as exploratory, experimental, and based on intuitive reasoning rather than being seen as a purely logical analytical process. He suggests various steps to "create order out of chaos". These steps will involve us in different ways of thinking, particularly about:

- the meaning of control, which he suggests should be based on self-organised behaviour that can be in a state of control without any one person controlling it
- power, which he describes as exerting authority by intervening with suggestions, and by providing a legit-

imation for open questioning and the creative use of argument and conflict

- cultural diversity, which he emphasises as being of value because of the different challenge that difference brings
- focus and purpose on ambiguous challenges rather than on clear long-term objectives or visions
- stretching situations, which he sees as a positive rather than negative
- the importance of group learning skills. Stacey suggests that this includes the habit of questioning beliefs and altering existing mental models
- creating resource slack. In terms of your individual situation, this means including time to reflect and develop strategic learning as a key priority.

This can be a useful approach especially if it is recognised that in many ways it reflects our everyday reality; and in this sense it is not new. Its newness is its use as a way of management thinking. The risk is that this will be taken as a new "flavour of the month" or recipe for success, rather than a way of engaging in a straightforward way with what is happening around us.

You may find it interesting to review where your thinking lies, in the areas of control, power, difference, focus and purpose, stretching situations, questioning beliefs and altering your existing mental models, and giving yourself some slack time. The chapter on systems thinking links with the ideas in this chapter.

Jerry Rhodes (1991), in his book *Conceptual Toolmaking* suggests that our thinking moves along strategic continua, continually seeking a balance, for instance, between cost and gain, reality and our ideal, self and others, short term and long term, caution and risk. This gives us another example of the necessity for non-linear thinking in complex or ambiguous situations.

Most people are perfectly able to think in a non-linear way, but they may not be aware of their ability or value it. It may feel as if we are being unclear or "woolly". It feels harder to pin down, to know that we are doing it. "Mapping" techniques, where the different elements of a situation are laid out with their interconnections, in a pictorial or diagrammatic form, can reassure us of our ability, and can surface the important interconnectedness that we are in fact aware of. Mind-maps are one example of this. It may require some "unlearning" for people who have been trained or educated in a setting dominated by logical and linear assumptions, but in my experience the ability is always there.

An interesting piece of research is described in *Opening Pandora's Box*, (Gilbert and Mulkay, 1984) where research scientists were interviewed about how they arrived at a certain set of findings; then the interview was compared with what the scientists had written describing the same research in learned journals. In the narrative, there were many incidental or coincidental happenings which led to the discovery, a looped, sometimes rather haphazard process. In the "official" version, the process was described as logical and sequential, the "scientific method". Both versions were probably an aspect of the truth, but the non-linear aspect, although probably the most creative, has less credibility and a description of it might not be published in the scientific press.

The guru's questions

In terms of clarifying your own thinking and your own work you might want to consider the "guru's questions", thinking them through in relation to yourself. For instance:

What do I contribute? What "business" are we/am I in? Where are we/am I going? (Drucker)

What makes me unique? How am I going to develop this uniqueness? (Porter)

What distinctive competencies do I have? What do I need to be good at to do my work successfully? (Hamel and Prahalad)

How do I decide about using my/our resources of money, buildings and people? (Boston Consulting Group)

Where am I in relation to our environment, stakeholders, aspirations and capabilities? (Egan, Mintzberg etc.)

What are the different possible futures facing me? What do I need to do to prepare for them? (Schwarz)

How do I actually make strategies? What small steps can I take? (Quinn)

How can I spot and reinforce effective "strategies" that I am using or that are already developing inside the organisation? How can I make best use of patterns in the organisation and the environment? (Minzberg)

How do I develop strategies in times of unpredictable and chaotic environments? How do I control myself and my part of the organisation in these times? (Stacey)

How do I reconcile the apparently opposing options facing me and my part of the organisation? (Hampden-Turner)

Conclusion

As a basis for managing multiple priorities with less stress, this chapter suggests that you take a close look at the way you think about things, particularly when under pressure. Having noticed your thought patterns, you are freer to streamline your thinking so that it supports what you are doing rather than slowing you up or absorbing the energy you need in order to cope. This may involve:

- using more appropriate language

- facing up to exaggerated fears or "rules" and amending them

- using your intuitive potential as well as your logical thinking and linking the two; revisiting your overall purpose and thinking strategically even about local or short-term matters.

It is also important to be aware of and value your ability to think in a non-linear way, responding to unpredictability and interconnectedness. The chapter on systems has more material about this.

2 Using project management thinking to increase your effectiveness

Introduction

- In many organisations, work is increasingly arranged around "projects" – fixed-term assignments with a team drawn together for the life of the project. Even without this being formally the case, much of our work and indeed our leisure activity includes dealing with multiple priorities, complex and/or numerous tasks, deadlines, constant communication across organisational boundaries and limited resources. Project management techniques are highly relevant in these circumstances. You can use project management methods to build a house or a boat, arrange a wedding, write a novel, or plan a holiday or a career change.

- In any task that is complex, that involves crossing functional boundaries, or that involves working with people over whom you do not have direct authority, then a project management approach will stand you in good stead.

- This chapter will take you through the project management approach, seen as a set of skills, styles and techniques, which will help you to achieve appropriate results without using inappropriate amounts of energy, time and other resources. The ideas apply to your current projects if you have them. You can also consider your work in general as if it were a project and use these approaches.

Some definitions

Project management is the planning, organising, directing and controlling of people and resources for a relatively short-term objective. It is established to accomplish a set of specific goals and objectives with a specific deadline by utilising a fluid approach.

A project is an undertaking that has a beginning and an end and is carried out to meet established goals within agreed objectives. Project management brings together and optimises the resources necessary to complete the project successfully.

What skills are involved in project management?

You need to be aware of what skills you need at particular times in managing your project and to be able to bring them into play appropriately. You can probably work them out for yourself; generally they are said to include:

- communicating, both sending and receiving information
- organising work flow to meet deadlines
- working with the organisational style, though knowing when to be different
- leadership and management
- knowing when to focus on the "customers" of the project and/or the "suppliers" of the project
- knowing when to focus on yourself and your own contribution
- understanding and resolving conflict
- building and supporting an effective team
- managing the resources involved and their flow
- managing your own energy and time.

Above all, you need the skill of rigorous and robust front-end thinking about:

- the purpose and desired outcomes of the project or piece of work

- what the investment of time, energy and resources is meant to achieve. "Why are we doing this?" "How will we know it's worked?" "What will it take to achieve this?"
- what the opportunity cost is: what are you not doing when you are carrying out this project or doing this work?

This kind of "front-end thinking" is probably the most important way in which project management thinking contributes to managing your time and energy creatively.

The summary plan

A summary plan of the project's essential elements enables you to tell at a glance what needs to be done, why and how, and when deliverables must be ready.

A typical summary plan, or project brief, might contain:

- statement of overall goal
- your responsibilities and where they end (the boundaries)
- other people's responsibilities. Organisational responsibility structure if relevant
- critical path – what needs to be done, by when. Key tasks and dates, giving you a milestone schedule
- overall budget – money and resources available, budget-holders and decision-makers, budgeting dates
- people in the project network – who connects with whom
- possible impact of the project on other people, departments or groups
- possible problems, obstacles etc. and what steps will be taken to deal with them.

activity

2.1

Step 1   *Think of a "simple" project: something such as cooking a family meal, planning your holiday, organising your desk.*

Step 2   *Test the flexibility and responsiveness of your thinking, by writing a summary plan for the project in the way outlined above.*

Result   *The activity has the effect of streamlining your approach. Working in this way means that you almost unconsciously get the pacing and timing of any enterprise right.*

Project accountability structure

The typical project or piece of work, even a small one, can degenerate into a mess of mismatched accountabilities, which can lead to confusion and blame. It is worth spending considerable time on discussing and clarifying accountability and authority in all parts and levels of the project. What are you responsible and accountable for, who else has responsibility or authority, what are the boundaries and where are the areas of overlap? With the project team, if you have one, spend time in clarifying the responsibilities and targets of each member. Even if you are working with a more general group of people, formally or informally, this process is worth investing in at an early stage. In this way you can avoid the "Why didn't you . . . ?", "Didn't you realise . . . ?" moments which can use up time and energy for no good effect.

Clarifying performance expectations or desired outcomes: resisting the activity trap

It is essential to establish clear performance expectations. You may be in a position to do this for yourself, unilaterally; in general, the other people involved, the stakeholders, need to be taken into account: what are their expectations, expressed in *their* terms?

It is tempting to focus on the project's tasks, instead of doing the hard thinking necessary to define the measurable or recognisable results the project should achieve. This is the "activity trap". Are you tempted by this? Does it seem easier to "get on with it" rather than think it through, consult with others and get a robust plan? One reason that any project, however large or small, gets stuck, fades away or fails is because there is no clear vision of the end result. And, in the absence of clear direction, accountability is impossible to measure.

How will you measure or recognise success at the end of this project or piece of work? What do you really expect to achieve for the time, effort and, perhaps, money that will be spent? Getting answers to these questions forces the kind of conceptual thinking that is the major priority at the beginning. With answers to these questions, which includes answers from the key people that will be affected by the end result, you are in a better position to drive the project towards the agreed upon measures of success. Without them, you are not in a position to deal with the subtle changes in expectations that you or other stakeholders develop as the project proceeds, nor in a position to measure success. Often when involved in a complex enterprise, we have an uneasy sense that "the goal posts have moved"; alternatively we may achieve the goal and yet various participants say or imply "Yes, but that wasn't really what we wanted". This will happen less with a regular routine of reviewing the success criteria, reminding people of them and adjusting them if necessary.

The success definition is *not* that you or the team will have carried out certain activities; it is to achieve a recognisable and preferably measurable result or outcome. If you fall into the trap of focusing on activities, you will not discover what the sponsor or stakeholders, or even you yourself, really want to "buy" or achieve until it is too late to refocus.

Finding out how stakeholders, the people involved and the people who mind about what happens, will recognise or measure a project's success at the end is not an easy task. The measurement or even the recognisable desired outcome is never just a budget and due date. You will often find that you or the project's initiator have not thought through what success will look like in detail, but have focused on the activities to be carried out.

Defining success criteria

Some results are measurable. Some are not measurable but can be recognised. Good specification of what you will recognise as success increases the likelihood of success by several factors.

"Provide the best possible customer service", or "Have a lovely wedding" are examples of an unmeasurable end result. You cannot measure or even recognise whether or not you have achieved this, if you have not discussed with your customers what they see as good or excellent service, or with bride and groom and other members of the family what they see as a lovely wedding.

A suggested result of "Answer 95 per cent of our customers' calls within 120 seconds", is measurable and quantifiable. It may provoke the useful arguments ("No, that's not what I mean") that in the end lead to a more solid definition that users of the project can agree on as being a satisfactory as well as a measurable end result. A suggested result of "Have a wedding where everyone feels comfortable, there is an atmosphere of celebration, and no more than the agreed money is spent" for example, is recognisable and provides a clearer benchmark for various decisions than "Have a lovely wedding".

Five aspects of project management

2.2

It is easy to assume that project management is basically good scheduling. While this is very important, it falls down unless it is backed up by four other activities. These can be summarised as specifying Managing, Coordinating, and Monitoring and Controlling.

Step 1   *Looking back on the work you were involved in during the last two months, select a small project or limited piece of work for which you had some responsibility.*

Step 2   *Assess yourself on your strengths in each area by reviewing how much attention you paid to each of the following:*

- *Specifying: what effort did you make, and how effective were you in being clear about such questions as "What will success look like to me? Who else will be affected? What are their criteria?"*
- *Scheduling: what attention did you pay to linking tasks in a logical order, planning to get and give information in an orderly fashion, being aware of time scales.*
- *Managing: how much of your energy was devoted to leading, coaching, supporting and delegating.*
- *Coordinating: what was your record in bringing together different aspects of the work, connecting other people together, maintaining a sense of the whole project in your own mind and charting all the people involved and understanding the network.*
- *Monitoring and controlling: how did you manage the business of checking whether things were on track, reviewing "is it working?", keeping records of decisions and actions, and responding and adapting to change.*

Result   *Using this checklist routinely for yourself means that you will improve your ability to manage more complex pieces of work. It will also give you an indication of what you need to get better at.*

Who is in my team?

In order to manage and coordinate effectively, you need to have a clear picture of the people involved, and how their contribution, their priorities and personal goals will affect the success of the project.

The effective project manager develops an awareness of the essential synergies between members of the team, and between the team and others whose actions are crucial to the success of the project. This may include the people with the power to make decisions about the project: the budget-holders – the people who are spending money; participants or people affected by the end result; those who are supplying essentials to the project; and those who are advising you. These considerations are worth bearing in mind in your work in general as well.

2.3

If you have a current or projected project or complex piece of work:

Step 1   *List everyone with whom you will be in contact and whose actions will contribute to success or failure.*

Step 2   *Think about each person individually:*

- ○ *What is their key contribution?*
- ○ *What do you need from them?*
- ○ *What motivates them?*
- ○ *What are their unique qualities or ways of contributing?*
- ○ *What other responsibilities do they have, apart from this project?*

Step 3   *Write down what you currently do to keep everyone informed and involved.*

Step 4   *Decide on some small ways in which you could improve what you do.*

Step 5   *After working this through, write down the key points emerging from this activity, and put in diary dates for meetings, for getting more information about the people involved, for consulting with key individuals, and for getting and giving information.*

Result   *This activity will streamline your communication and enrich your relationships with the people you need to be connected with.*

Developing the critical path

A critical path is the order in which work is done in the most economical and satisfactory way. A good critical path has no bottlenecks and makes sure everything is ready for each succeeding step. A computer scientist running a degree programme described the critical path to her students as the mental processes used in preparing a three-course meal effectively, including having the gravy hot at the end.

2.4 Developing a critical path backwards

You can use your summary plan (described above), and your review of the people involved (also described above), to develop a critical path plan, working back from the endpoint, that is, the end result and deadline for the project.

It is best to work this out on a whiteboard, or any large area where you can erase and modify, until all the necessary steps and branches have been taken into account. It is preferable to do this "live", with one or two others, friends or colleagues, who may notice steps you have missed.

Step 1   *As already discussed, be very clear about the **final result** or **product**, with its date, describing it and your final activity in realistic detail. Describe the dates realistically, e.g. "Presentation to Board on . . .", "Pilot by users on . . .", "Full implementation on . . .", "Draft to publishers on . . .", or "Wedding on . . . at . . . with x guests, to well-catered and smooth running reception at . . .".*

Step 2   *Then, starting from the end result or product, write down the essential immediate prerequisites (and the prerequisites for the* *prerequisites) for the end result to have taken place. The phrase "which means that" is of great use here. For example: "By December 19. . . X must have happened, which means that by . . . (date) . . . I (or someone else) must have . . . which will require Z to have happened by (date). This means that I must . . . on (date)."*

Be sure to include people you need to speak to and information you need to share. You will quickly move into branches and loops, and this is the stage to be aware of them.

Step 3   *Having done this, you are in a position to identify key tasks in a logical order. Notice which actions are dependent on which other actions – a "dependency" – and build this into the plan. This may mean drawing links between strands. Identify lag time or slack time when you are waiting for one thing to happen but could be doing something else. Then check that the general flow makes sense.*

Step 4   *You are now ready to put in realistic milestones – key dates for actions. You should also add in dates for monitoring: dates when you will refer to the plan to check progress.*

Step 5   *Then discuss the plan with an outsider as a reality check. Encourage them to ask you the naive questions like "What will that involve?" "What needs to be in place for that to happen?" "How long will that take?" "What if . . .?"*

Step 6   *At this stage there are two more essential steps. **Do not omit them**. Put **all** dates in your diary and communicate the plan and dates to all individuals whose contribution is essential, and check that these dates also work for them. Their response may mean modifying the plan. It is unrealistic to load unachievable expectations on people over whom you may have minimal influence.*

Result   *The key to success lies in the "working backwards" approach, starting from the end date and specified desired outcome or result, making sure that each action or event is backed up by a realistic* *set of previous actions that are necessary for it to be successful. This avoids the "activity trap", keeps the focus on what is to be achieved by when, and brings into focus things that might be left out in a "forward planning" approach. This activity helps you plan realistically in a more creative way. With this kind of plan, the "people" issues which can often slow down a project are properly taken care of.*

We can see a critical path is a series of interconnected events, together making up a complex chain. The weakest link in that chain can be described as the system's constraint. Improvements elsewhere in the chain will make no difference unless the weakest link is also improved. The "backwards" approach helps you identify the weakest link or constraint, so that you can focus energy and resources to prevent this link being a constraint on the whole system. In some cases the weakest link or constraint is not inside your organisational frame or your control. If this is the case you may need either to widen your frame and put resources into the weak place, or accept the constraint. If you accept it, you may realise that you are putting inappropriate energy or resources into other parts of the system. This may mean adjusting the critical path. This kind of approach is described in the novel entitled *The Goal* (Goldratt and Cox, 1995).

I used this approach with some of the team managers who were taking their teams to the Olympics in Atlanta, a complex and demanding process. Their goal at this stage was "get the team to Atlanta in a position to perform to their personal best". More than sheer logistics was included: personal issues, idiosyncrasies, the situation in Atlanta, time for acclimatisation, all needed to be taken into account. We went through this process "live" on a whiteboard with one of the most effective team managers. As he talked this through he gained insights he needed that his already very effective forward planning had omitted to take into account. For example, one of his subgoals was to get the team to the USA early so that they could get a sense of the environment they were going to compete in. This involved getting them time off work prior to the Olympics itself. His teams all had full-time jobs, so it involved either him or the competitors talking to their managers at work, to negotiate agreement for the time away. This in turn involved deciding who was the most appropriate person to have the conversation, and making time to plan how to present the case, and making an appointment to see the managers involved. All of this needed to be in the diary. Other team managers who watched the process as we did it "live" were struck by things that they should have already done. One team manager, who was in fact at the workshop as a preparation for bringing a new sport to the following Olympics in five years' time began to realise that there were things she should already be doing.

What if? Conflict, dilemmas and risk management

In any project or complex piece of work there will be expected and unexpected conflict and also decisions involving risk. Before you get into a project or new piece of work it is important to think where the conflicts may lie. You can learn a great deal by discovering where the conflicts of interest lie for you, for the other people immediately involved and for other stakeholders. As well as conflicts of interest, it is worth looking at where the conflicts of personalities may lie. This is not just the tendency to have arguments – differing personalities have a different approach to the world; we see the world in different ways. Different assumptions may be present among the people involved. There may, for example, be different views about how a project like this should be effected; about the relative importance of this piece of work; about the importance, indeed, of work itself as compared with family life; about the micropolitics of the situation; about the long-term as opposed to the short-term issues.

You may find it useful to look at your own ways of understanding and dealing with conflict, and how you compare in this respect with the other people involved. Some people see conflict as something to be avoided at all cost; others see it as a valuable way of clearing the air, understanding the situation and moving forward; others again as a way of forcing through their own ideas and methods. These differences can be a creative force in your enterprise, when acknowledged and valued. If not acknowledged, however, they can slow things up, lead to undercurrents and game playing.

2.5 How do you deal with conflict?

Step 1 *Look back at the last four weeks and find three moments of actual or potential conflict, when you were in disagreement with someone else. Give each moment a number, 1, 2 or 3.*

Step 2 *In each case, consider what may really have been underlying the conflict. Use Table 2.1.*

Table 2.1 Sources of conflict

	Situation 1	Situation 2	Situation 3
Power	☐	☐	☐
Resources	☐	☐	☐
Ways of doing things	☐	☐	☐
Different goals or purposes	☐	☐	☐
Different personalities	☐	☐	☐

Step 3 *Consider how you react in each case.*

Step 4 *Consider how you actually behaved. What did you do?*

Step 5 *Consider what you would see as a good outcome to this conflict or disagreement, in the short term and long term.*

Step 6 *Being as honest with yourself as you possibly can, reflect on what you typically feel and do when you do not get your own way or get what you want.*

Result *The first step to being able to handle conflict creatively is to understand what it is about for you. Do not jump too quickly into making assumptions about what it means for the other person. This* *activity gives you a moment to reflect on your own patterns, and what may trigger you into a conflict situation. Being more aware of this you can manage conflict rather than being engulfed in it or avoiding it.*

There is more about managing conflict in Chapter 4.

Risk management

Risk management involves looking at the possible outcomes of something going wrong at every stage of the project or piece of work, and working those through. You might begin, for example, by exploring the risk of not completing the piece of work, or consider what might happen if this project were not done at all.

Drawing out a risk management matrix can be helpful. This involves comparing aspects of the project with factors that can affect them; considering which aspect is prone to which risk; deciding who is responsible for managing that risk; and drawing up an overall risk management strategy. This strategy gives you a framework for where to put your attention, how and to whom to delegate, and in general a wider and more intelligent view of the project or piece of work. Table 2.2 gives you the kind of matrix. Table 2.3 shows you an example drawn up by someone managing a project connected with personal pensions in a financial institution.

This can give you a more focused understanding of areas where conflict and risk are likely, and where you need to be particularly careful.

Thinking of a project as an investment: making the business case

Even in a small personal project or piece of work it is worth working out the perceived gain, proportional to the investment involved. What are you investing in terms of

Table 2.2 Risk factors affecting aspects of the project

Risk factors that can affect each aspect

Aspects of project				

time, money, or alternatives excluded, by taking this on? What is the organisation investing, in terms of time and in terms of other resources? This can also help you to prioritise.

What will be the gain when the project or piece of work is completed? The reasons for taking it on and committing the resources may be tangible (expressed for instance in financial terms), but less tangible factors such as future viability, personal satisfaction and social value may also be present. The intangible factors may actually constitute the return on investment that is being looked for, even though they are hard to quantify. In many cases, they are the real drivers of

USING PROJECT MANAGEMENT THINKING TO INCREASE YOUR EFFECTIVENESS

Table 2.3 Risk factors example

Aspects of project, e.g.		Risk factors that can affect each aspect, e.g.					
		Illness	Computer crash	Takeover or merger	Change in staff	Change in legislation	Change in funding
Key personnel Me		✓			✓		✓
Jack			✓		✓		✓
Jane					✓		✓
Stakeholder Head of department				✓			
Stakeholder Regulatory body						✓	
Computer hardware and software			✓				✓

investment of time and resources, even where there is a clear tangible financial gain. For example, the results of a project for developing the marketing of a new product can be directly measured in terms of increased sales and profitability, and success may result in a bonus; but in many cases the people involved in the project are investing their time to achieve prestige, longer-term success, career opportunities. That is the return on investment that they are looking for. The company, too, is looking for security and long-term viability (intangibles), and is seeking to increase market share (tangible) in order to achieve these.

Case studies: two different types of project in practice

This is an example of a difficult project that was carried out by a group of people in a transport organisation who already had demanding jobs in the organisation. It had to be carried out alongside the other work they were doing. It was a "Make or Buy" research project: "make or buy" in terms of the decision as to whether they should buy in engineering expertise or continue to provide their own; providing recommendations based on quantified data which had to be collected by the project group. Interviewed about the features that made the project successful, Harvey Robinson said, "keep everyone involved: be clear to them about what is needed and trust them to do it". I was involved in a small way, as one of Harvey's strategies was to have an outsider facilitate the process of their two-monthly review meetings so that he could concentrate on the content, review and planning. Another of his strategies was to choose highly capable people who had the particular skill and know-how to carry out a specific aspect of the project.

In his experience of managing projects in a financial institution, Glenn Blackman of Barclays Commercial Services Limited found that the difference between successful and unsuccessful project management lay particularly in two areas. "The most important things are:

- to involve and inform all the stakeholders, particularly the ones who have the power to affect or challenge your result, and
- to divide the project which seems huge and unmanageable into small manageable steps, but still keep the whole picture in mind."

Even those of us who are not carrying out major projects can use this kind of thinking.

2.6 Self-assessment: what are your strengths and weaknesses in project management thinking?

Which of the following do you excel at?
Which if improved might make your life easier?
Which if improved would make you more effective?
Which are irrelevant to your current or future work?

1. *Communications*
   - *choosing appropriate information to send*
   - *sending it to the right people*
   - *at the right time*
   - *seeking actively the information you need for yourself.*

2. *Organising work flow to meet deadlines.*

3. *Working with the organisational style, though knowing when to be different.*

4. *Knowing when to focus on the "customers" of the project and/or the "suppliers" of the project.*

5. *Accepting and resolving conflict.*

6. *Building and supporting an effective team; being aware of who is involved on the margins.*

7. *Managing the resources involved and their flow.*

8. *Rigorous and robust front-end thinking*
   - *about the purpose and desired outcomes of the project; "Why are we doing this?" "How will we know it's worked?" "What will it take to achieve this?"*

- *about the investment of time, money and other resources; how to manage and monitor the use of resources*
- *understanding the opportunity cost: "What is not done when I do this? What is the price of doing this? What will it cost me or others, and how will I know if it's worth it?"*

9. *Critical path planning.*

10. *Defining success criteria.*

Conclusion

Complex pieces of work, especially where there is a pressure to achieve an end result by a certain time, and where there are competing priorities, can be managed effectively by taking a project management approach. This involves spending time on developing and getting agreement about success criteria and desirable outcomes for yourself and among the stakeholders or key players, and revisiting these as the work or project progresses. Valuing the contribution of others involved in the work, and getting a sense of their style and priorities, helps you to manage the inevitable conflict in a creative and productive way. Developing a critical path, where the flow of the work and the interdependencies between different strands of the work is made clear, is an essential part of the process. This path, including the timings involved, must be shared fully with other members of the working team. Understanding where are the constraints, the weak links or bottlenecks is essential, as is understanding the amount of energy to be spent on strengthening the weak links to get a balanced flow. Reviewing where you are and being free to adjust within the agreed boundaries of time, money and other resources, requires a combination of clear purpose and flexibility which is the main component of project management thinking.

3 Prioritising intelligently realistically and proactively

Introduction

- Many people these days have too many things to do, so traditional prioritising and time management in itself will not deal with everything that has to be done. For people in this situation prioritising takes on a different kind of flavour. It means deciding which things are least damaging not to do, balancing between long-term gain and short-term gain, and spending sufficient time to decide what is really urgent and what can be put off or be done by somebody else. It means making tougher decisions based on values and career and life goals. These decisions are in effect choices, and making intelligent choices in a complex world requires information, intuition and the ability to see a bigger picture.

Using this chapter

This chapter will take you through thoughts and activities about prioritising and goal-setting, linking them to your own values. These activities are useful and enriching. Beware of turning your life into a "project" however. The final section of this chapter "Living without goals" provides a useful balance.

What is important?

The important/not important, urgent/not urgent matrix is a good starting point. I have found Steven Covey's (1992) chapter on managing your priorities in *The Seven Habits of Highly Effective People* helpful.

Activities can be put into a familiar matrix, of what you consider to be important or not, urgent or not (see Table 3.1).

Table 3.1 The priorities matrix

	Urgent	*Not urgent*
Important	1 Crises Pressing problems Deadline-driven projects near their deadline	4 Planning, strategic thinking Prevention Improving capability Developing relationships Recognising new opportunities
Not important	2 Interruptions, some calls Some mail, some reports Some meetings Proximate, pressing matters Popular activities	3 Trivia, busy work Some mail Some phone calls Time wasters Pleasant activities

What happens when you focus primarily on one quadrant?

1. The urgent and important quadrant.
   Focusing entirely or mainly on this quadrant, can lead to crisis management, always putting out fires, stress and burnout. People focusing here lose touch completely with their longer-term goals, and forget to consider the kind of life they really want, or the kind of work they aspire to. People may find themselves focusing on this kind of work because dealing with such urgent things gives them a sense of importance. The "adrenalin high" can become something of an addiction. As well as stress and burnout, working mainly in this quadrant can leave a long-term problem in that their individual sense of worth is very bound up in the fire-fighting.

2. The urgent though not important quadrant.

   Feeling constrained to act mainly in this quadrant leads to short-term focus, crisis management, feelings of being a victim and out of control. In this state, goals and plans seem worthless. Circumstances of work, the working style of the organisation or society itself, may push people into this way of living and working. It is hard for people in this situation to find time to reflect and think, and at least have a rich inner life, even if externally there may seem to be few choices. Some people manage to do this, by detaching themselves from their work situation.

3. The not urgent and not important quadrant.

   Spending a lot of time in activities in this quadrant can be the result of too much stress, and can be a useful warning sign that your work situation is not right for you. Although spending inappropriate amounts of time on these activities reduces the value of one's work, used in a balanced way they are, when chosen, a useful antidote to the "serious" approach to work people may take in other quadrants.

4. The important but not urgent quadrant.

   These activities are easy to leave "until there's time". Focusing on these activities, however, can lead to fewer crises, a better sense of balance, vision and perspective. Many "urgent but not important" activities can be altered by including longer-term goals (such as building alliances or improving relationship skills) when doing things which might be seen otherwise to be unimportant, such as attending irrelevant meetings.

If you really need to manage more with less, you will put serious energy and commitment into activities that are "important but not urgent", having first of all had a serious look at your priorities, both short and long term, and the context you are in.

There are various ways of improving one's own situation, using this matrix.

Covey (1992) suggests a useful question:

What is one thing in my personal and professional life that if I did on a regular basis, would make a tremendous positive difference?

PRIORITISING INTELLIGENTLY REALISTICALLY AND PROACTIVELY

When you have answered this question which, when you stop and think, is not hard to do, look at the proportion of time you currently spend on this activity.

The only place to get time for Quadrant 2 activities is from 3 and 4. We cannot ignore the urgent and important activities of Quadrant 1, although it will shrink in size as we spend more time in prevention. To say "yes" to Quadrant 2 activities, we have to say "no" to Quadrant 3 and 4.

To manage our lives with more place for important but not urgent activities, Covey suggests that we should organise on a weekly basis, and schedule our priorities rather than prioritising our schedule. He suggests that we look at our whole life, and use steps like the following:

3.1

Step 1   *Identify all the roles or commitments that are important to you, in work and in home life.*

Step 2   *Select two or three important results for each role or commitment in the next seven days. Some of these should be goals which will bring your long-term objectives nearer.*

Step 3   *Decide a time that you will allocate to these commitments or goals.*

Step 4   *Put these times into the weekly diary, linking them where possible to other necessary activities.*

Step 5   *Alter or delegate "urgent" activities so that they achieve longer-term goals, as well as the shorter-term goals that make them urgent, and keep making sure that your activities match your underlying values and principles.*

Like most management writers, Covey makes it look easy and also simple. In my experience, most people's lives are more fuzzy and complicated than that. None the less, in general his approach is worth considering if only because he encourages us to think about our values and our real priorities, allowing work to take its proper part in our lives.

What makes things urgent?

It is worth looking at what gets activities into the urgent box. You may have some assumptions that need checking about what *has* to be done urgently. Some of the activities in Chapter 1 may be useful here, as it is possible that your habits of thinking may be getting in the way of making appropriate choices for yourself.

3.2

A list of situations follows; think about how you yourself respond or might respond in similar situations, and what for you triggers a sense of urgency.

Step 1 *Use these hypothetical situations to help you get a clearer picture of how something gets to the top of your "Do it now!" list.*

a. *The phone is ringing while you are spending some time sorting out a problem. You interrupt what you are doing to answer it, thus treating it as urgent. What is the thinking behind this decision?*

b. *Your boss asks you to do something today "as a matter of urgency". You drop what you are doing, and comply with your boss's request, thus treating it as urgent. What are the thoughts that trigger this response?*

c. *The fire alarm rings and you leave your office in the middle of a phone call and go to the designated collecting area. What are your reasons?*

d. You are completing a project and the deadline is today, so you stay at work until 10.00 p.m. to finish it, thus missing a family occasion. What is the process by which one requirement gets prioritised over the other?

e. A person who gets very aggressive when not satisfied rings you for some information which they genuinely need. You prefer to deal with it now, although it is inconvenient for you, rather than put up with their bad temper. What are the reasons for this choice?

f. You have a pet which gets suddenly ill; you take it to the vet, thus missing an urgent meeting at work. Reasons?

Step 2   Review what you have learned about the way you appear to prioritise. Do you have similar real-life examples? If someone only observed your choices of action, what would they assume about your values and priorities?

3.3 What gets in the way?

Step 1   Which of these get in the way of your effectiveness in the sense that they use up more time or energy than you would like? Ring the appropriate letter.

a. Not sticking to agenda at meetings
b. Inability to shorten/terminate calls
c. No standards of performance
d. Dealing only with urgent matters
e. Postponing unpleasant tasks
f. Fear of causing offence.

a. No decisions from meetings
b. Irrelevant "chat" at meetings
c. Actions not followed up

d. Overlooking consequences of decisions
e. Lack of self-discipline
f. Finger in every pie.

a. Meetings too long
b. Unstructured telephone conversations
c. Ambiguous instructions
d. Lack of overview/perspective
e. Doing things "at the last minute"
f. "I would rather **do** than **think**".

a. Not challenging time-wasting at meetings
b. Inability to shorten/terminate visits from others
c. No deadlines
d. Not following things up
e. Doing things "at the last minute"
f. Over-reacting to all difficulties.

a. Poorly organised and chaired meetings
b. Frequent interruptions
c. Too much routine work
d. Getting taken off course by emergencies
e. Poor communication channels
f. "I always feel under pressure".

Any others?

Step 2   *Scoring and tips for improvement*

High "a"   Manage your role in meetings better.
High "b"   Time yourself to five minutes for each call or chat.
High "c"   Some of these are beyond your control. Work with
           things you have control over. This may include
           delegating.
High "d"   Improve your strategic thinking and strategic behaviour;
           keep your eye on the overall aim of what is being done.

High "e"   *Get someone to help you organise yourself and use your diary better.*

High "f"   *Review your emotional state and your dependence on others' approval.*

Step 3   *Choose three of the items on the list that you would like to do something about.*

Step 4   *Make a list of what you will do **from today** to cut down their ability to reduce your effectiveness.*

Result   *Getting a fuller understanding of your own weak spots in letting things get in the way of your effectiveness helps you be more proactive in dealing with them.*

Setting appropriate success criteria

It is impossible to prioritise realistically unless you are able to keep reminding yourself of what your overall priorities really are, and what achieving those priorities would look like. It is useful to ask yourself questions like:

- How will I know I am succeeding?
- What are my criteria for success?
- What is the desired outcome in observable results of what I am doing?
- Who decides what counts as success? Is it my boss, is it shareholders, or is it me?

These are important things to sort out in your own mind.

It is also important to look at how you decide what is good enough. There is a saying: "Good enough is good enough." It is important to be able to decide the appropriate level at which you will provide results, that is, the right amount of detail, the right amount to be delivered to satisfy what is required and be manageable within the time scale.

Many of us are in the habit of trying to achieve excellence in everything we do. These days, realistically, that is not possible. Choosing which things you will focus on to deliver in total excellence, and which things realistically only need to be "good enough" is an important energy-saving activity. Developing this skill leads to greater effectiveness.

3.4

This may seem rather an odd activity. It certainly mirrors many situations in everyday life. Trying it makes you think in a different way.

Step 1
Choose three things, tasks, activities or projects, in which you are currently strongly involved.

Step 2
Imagine that only one of those three can be delivered absolutely 100 per cent; one can be delivered let's say 80 per cent to satisfy whoever it is for, and one activity can be delivered at only 50 per cent of the total possibility. How would you decide which would get the 100 per cent and which the 50 per cent?

Step 3
Notice your criteria for deciding.

It is always worth writing down (as we suggested in Chapter 2) what you will be recognising when the job, or the part of the job you are currently involved in, is done. Often when we are involved in a heavy workload of many different kinds of work we are so busy doing the work that we forget to spend time thinking about what we are trying to achieve here. Even more importantly we forget to write down what we are trying to achieve, with a time scale, so that we can keep a track of what we are trying to do.

It is also important to be very clear about what things are so clearly unachievable, that it is not worth spending any time on them. Whatever you do they would not be achieved. In this way you can begin to develop a priority schedule of what you are going to put your energy into and what you are not. It is not possible for most people to put all their energy into everything they have committed to; setting realistic levels of result is a strategic approach to a heavy workload.

Separating important and unimportant in terms of risk

Possibly as you have been reading this you have been struck with a sense of risk. An important part of prioritising is the ability to balance the risk of selecting one activity or goal to prioritise over another. There is always an opportunity cost. What is the cost of having one thing as a high priority and focusing on that at the expense of other things? What is the risk of not doing something that does not seem to be high on your priority list?

activity **3.5**

It may be quite useful at this stage to do a decision tree including all the options for one of the items in your portfolio of work and what the risks are if you did them less well than you would like, or spent less time and resources on them than you would prefer to do.

The decision tree method

Step 1   *Choose a situation which you could prioritise as very important, less important or not important at all. Write down or discuss the outcomes of prioritising this situation in each of the three ways. Then draw out a tree of outcomes like that in Diagram 3.1.*

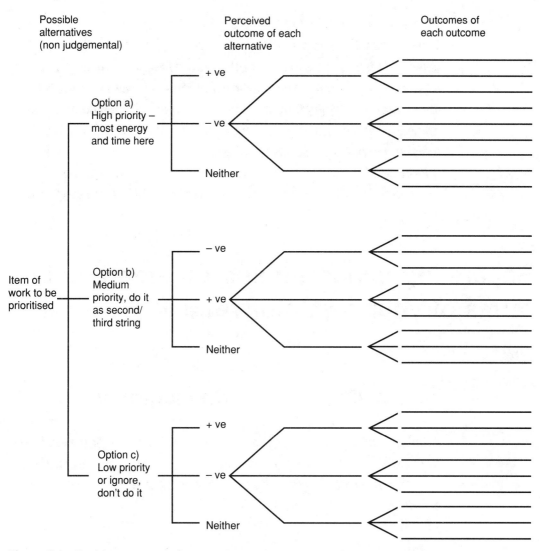

Figure 3.1 Decision tree example

Take a look at the longer-term consequences of each option, including any risks. Be sure to follow on from the risks: for instance, a risk might be "I won't meet X's deadline". Draw out the positive, negative and neutral outcomes of that risk, so that you can have a good clear look at reality, before deciding. Sometimes the short-term risk is not as serious as it seems; at other times, it is not only serious in itself, but leads to long-term consequences that are even more serious. Some options that have short-term positive outcomes, have long-term outcomes that are extremely negative.

This is particularly obvious in management and in industry: any companies that have prioritised down-sizing are now wondering where all their talent and corporate wisdom has gone, as well as the morale of the staff. It is certainly true in terms of industry's effects on the environment: things we do for short-term gain, often come around and surprise a company with long-term negative outcomes. It can be the same in one's personal life: seeing winning an argument as a priority can lead to a short-term feeling of satisfaction, and a quick win. In the long term it may leave you with enemies and a bad reputation.

Separating important and unimportant in terms of your own motivation

3.6 Looking at your own motivation

Another way to be sure you have allocated activities or goals to the right level of "important" or "unimportant" is to link them to your personal motivation. How does a particular activity meet your own priorities?

Step 1   *How would you prioritise the following "career values" for yourself?*

- ❍ *Meaning: doing things which you consider to be valuable for their own sake.*
- ❍ *Expertise: aiming to increase your expertise in your specialised field.*
- ❍ *Independence: seeking to be in an independent position, and be able to make key decisions for yourself.*
- ❍ *Security: looking for a solid and predictable future.*
- ❍ *Relationships: developing nourishing relationships at work.*

○ *Power or influence: working for the opportunity to exert influence and power over people and resources.*
○ *Material rewards: achieving a high standard of living, wealth or possessions.*

Considering which of these are the most important to you at the moment can give you a sense of direction, in terms of the aspects or qualities in yourself which you want to develop.

Step 2 *For example, you could take your highest priority and consider in what ways this is being satisfied at the moment by the way you are working. You could then move on to consider in what small ways you could increase your satisfaction in this area.*

Result *This activity helps you to review your priorities and to examine the way you choose one activity over another, in ways that move you towards your goals.*

When choosing what to do first, or deciding how to prioritise your time, look back at the list above, and see whether you are choosing authentically according to your own reasons for working. If you are not, it is worth reflecting on what it is that you *are* responding to, and on your own motivation for doing what you do. It is important to align your priorities with your motivation. If you are continually acting in ways that differ from what you say matters to you, it may be that you are not completely clear about what does in truth matter to you. There is more work on clarifying your values in Chapter 7, Activity 7.3.

Describing goals with accuracy

It is important to be very specific. Here is a routine that brings you much nearer to success than vagueness does.

1. State what your goal is in the positive; write down what you *do* want to be happening, rather than what you do not want to be happening.

PRIORITISING INTELLIGENTLY REALISTICALLY AND PROACTIVELY

2. Describe the context; be specific about with whom, where, and in what setting this will be happening.
3. Describe what it will be like when you succeed with this goal; what will the evidence be that you have achieved what you are looking for, what you are setting out to do? When it is working, what will you notice? What will other people notice?
4. Check that this aim or goal is within your control; if it is a goal that depends on other people for its achievement, then outline what your part in it is. This may include your subgoals about influencing other people who will contribute to the achievement of the main goal.
5. Be clear about gains and losses; it is important to check what you might lose if you achieve your goals. These can be the "invisible" features that make it unexpectedly hard to carry through to success. If you get a sense of what these are, it is easier to allow for them in your planning.

Having carried out this routine, you are now in a good position to review your priorities.

The "what if" approach

The strategic planner scans the horizon to see what trends are emerging and then begins to think about "what if . . ." situations, to address the trends that she or he sees. In the same way, the ability to take a look at the "unthinkable" possibilities, not in order to plan for them, but to be ready for the unexpected, is essential in an overcrowded life. Thinking the unthinkable can also help you to take a good look at your goals and priorities and take them to a deeper level. It can be easy to get swept up in a fashion, in what everyone else seems to be thinking, without taking stock of what you yourself (and the people you are near to) really want and value.

A manager I once worked with was caught up in a driven, high-pressured role that he said he disliked and that meant he hardly ever saw his family. When challenged, he explained: "I have to do this, to keep the kind of salary that supports my family in the lifestyle they want." I asked him how recently he had checked this out with his family, and a curious look came over his face. In quite a different voice, he said "I haven't ever discussed it with them". My unspoken question was "What if they would like to see you more and would be prepared to give up the big house and the ponies?" Another question might also be "What if you are losing contact with your wife and family to such an extent that you may lose them for good?" You do not always need to scan the horizon for trends; sometimes the trends are there, very close to home if only you look.

Using accurate language

When people describe their plans and goals, they often use rather weak and inaccurate language. "I'll try to . . .". What does that really mean? In what way does a person trying to do something look different from someone who is actually doing it? It is more useful to describe what will actually be happening that was not happening before, in very precise terms. Equally the phrase "From now on, I must . . ." is very weak in comparison with "From now on I will . . .".

Living with goals

Setting priorities means that you plan to do first things first. First things refers to the most important things, those that help you move closer to your goals, or that move you or keep you in the direction of your purpose. This means distinguishing between what *has* to be done, what *ought* to be done, what you want to do (if there is time), and what should be left undone.

activity

3.7 Life goals and priorities

Writing down your goals has a more powerful effect than dreaming them or saying them. We sometimes hold ourselves back from doing this, out of embarrassment, perhaps or a feeling that it is "tempting fate". It may be linked with our reluctance, in cultures such as the British, to ask for what we want, for fear of having the unpleasant experience of asking and not getting.

Step 1   *Give yourself some reflection time, consider what you dream of in life, and then write what comes to mind.*

Make sure that your wishes and goals come from the heart, and that you would welcome them and live them authentically if you attained them.

Step 2   *Notice what you experience as you write them down; is it pleasurable or uncomfortable?*

Step 3   *Then make a note of the small intermediate common-sense steps that might turn the goals into a reality.*

Step 4   *When you have listed the intermediate steps, put those steps in your diary: a more concrete way of turning dreams into actual experience. See exactly when you have to take action.*

Step 5   *If you share your goals with your friends and family you will feel more committed, although for some people it is important to keep their goals private to themselves.*

Step 6   *Review your goals from time to time so you can modify, add to or eliminate goals that no longer serve your needs. But whatever you do, do not let the life goals that are your basic priorities get lost amid the urgencies of everyday business.*

Living without goals

Goals can give a sense of purpose, and a standard against which to prioritise or make choices. The process of setting authentic goals for yourself is a powerful tool. There is another side to the story however. If you live your life totally in the metaphor of "achievable goals", however worthwhile those goals are, you run the risk of becoming a slave to that goal. Even if your goal is "balance in life", or "looking after myself", if you treat it as an ambition, you may lose the very goal you are looking for. As Ogilvy (1995) says in his book

Living without a Goal (p. 72) "a life enslaved to a single goal, no matter how noble, becomes a mechanism rather than an organism, a business plan rather than a biography" and can lose you the experience of "life lived in real time". The goal-focused approach can lead you to "overplanning your life, at the expense of living it". It can also blind you to the dynamic unpredictability of life, and leave you with the assumption that you should choose clarity and try to remove ambivalence, rather than living with both.

Conclusion

This chapter looks at ways of managing more of what you really want with less extraneous or unreflective activity. This means prioritising, which involves a hard look at what you are trying to achieve and how you are trying to live, and then sorting and choosing your activities so that they match at least loosely what you are trying to do and be. Clarity about goals, without being addicted to them, is an important part of this way of living, as is an understanding of your own feelings about risk and your own motivations. Thinking about the short term and the long term helps you maintain a balance in choosing your priorities.

4 Influencing without authority

Introduction

● As the explicit lines of power shift and become transformed in organisations, families and society in general, different ways of getting things done emerge. These rely on a different kind of power, a power to influence that does not rely on authority. A continuum can be observed. At one end, people operate manipulatively and covertly, without respect for the position of the other person or group; and at the other end they operate with transparency and integrity, in a way that takes a wider view of the outcome, and includes where possible a gain for all parties. Most influencing falls between these two extremes.

Using this chapter

This chapter discusses ways of getting more things done with less authority. This includes developing an awareness of the positions and priorities of the other people involved in any situation, being selective in your use of argument and developing an astuteness about the micropolitical context in which you are operating. This needs to be combined with a sense of your own desired outcomes. An unexpected result of working in this way is that your own priorities widen and become more inclusive. It can lead to developmental working relationships, rather than adversarial ones.

There are many techniques and skills that will make you more able to influence people over whom you have no authority;

ways of increasing your personal power, some of which this chapter will cover. Remember that unless you use them with a sense of integrity, of respect for other people, they will probably rebound on you.

It does not have to be difficult. Developing your personal power and your ability to influence others with integrity is a good example of how to manage more with less, of making things easy. Choosing the route of exploiting others may also be effective according to some criteria, but cannot be described as an example of managing more with less. It is rather an example of externalising your costs, of making others pay the price. We see it all around us, and we also see the unattractive and destructive long-term outcomes. The approach discussed in this chapter can give you more of the gains and fewer of the losses.

Influencing effectively without authority demands a high degree of self-awareness about your own purpose and values, an understanding of how different people react to your style, and the ability to balance your need for short-term success with your longer-term goals.

Understanding power and influence

Reflect for a moment on the people who you are inclined to help. Develop some ideas about what it is in them, or in what they do, that gets you to agree to do something for them. What is it that you respond to with agreement? Who around you behaves in such a way that you are willing to take on their priorities?

Consider the stories of two very different people, with very different influencing styles, experiencing a similar pattern of how things went for them.

I met a manager, Joe, who worked in an organisation where the climate was designed to be competitive and aggressive. Individual departments or projects had to compete with each other for resources. Everyone was under pressure. The most successful people were those who were driven by a need to get results and who were prepared to be very aggressive with others who did not meet deadlines. In keeping with this, Joe had developed a ruthless style that was very successful in achieving his short-term results, and had experienced rapid promotion. By the time I met him, however, he had got to the stage where it was not working for him; he had made a number of enemies along the way, who once out of his direct line of attack, were happy to drag their feet. He was not seen as "senior material" because of his tendency to upset people. This was a bitter realisation for him, particularly as he had been well rewarded for this kind of behaviour through his career up to now.

Another manager I met, Marilyn, had developed a high degree of political astuteness. She had a knack for understanding who held the reins of power, and who were the key decision-makers. Not only that, she had an ability to "tune in" to their position, and to choose a style of approach and language that they connected with and liked. This was very effective for her. Similarly to Joe, however, she came to a stage where it began to stop working for her. In her case it was because people developed a kind of mistrust for her, even though they liked meeting with her and working with her. "Who is the real Marilyn?" one of her colleagues asked me. I overheard someone else say "She's too good to be true". Gradually, like Joe, the very skill and aptitude that had worked for her began to work against her.

These examples show that there is not a fail-safe formula that lasts for ever for having influence or getting people to do what you want. In Joe's case, matching his behaviour with the climate and culture of the organisation worked well for a certain length of time, and pleased his seniors. After a while, the unattractive aspects of this behaviour, the effects it had on other people, began to work against him. With hindsight he realised that he had been very one-sided in his search for success. He had a strong caring ability in him which he had over-ridden in order to succeed. This left him feeling even worse when he realised that the aggressive behaviour, which in many ways had been hard for him, was not paying off in the longer term. This kind of thing often happens when people work against their own nature. They exaggerate the behaviour they are choosing, or do it with a kind of crassness and lack of finesse. Joe had been like this in his aggressive phase. When we met he was going through a re-evaluating process, which included finding ways to work that were more aligned with his own nature, and included building bridges to people whom he had hurt or offended.

In Marilyn's case, the kind of things people were beginning to say about her were things that she was even more inclined to say about herself. She had a real sense that she did not know who she was. All she had been focusing on was being the "right" person for those that she wanted to influence. When we met she was having to cope with a strong sense of being a fraud, of having lost her way, of despising the very skills and abilities that had brought her success in a difficult organisation. In fact, she was at heart a woman of great integrity. In a way similar to Joe, she had been working "against her own nature", and again had been rather one-sided in her approach. In Joe's case, he had not let others (or even himself) see his more caring and responsive side, only his apparently ruthless drive to succeed, regardless of the cost to others. Marilyn had not taken the opportunity to link her micropolitical skills with her honesty and integrity, but had almost set these aspects of her character aside in her successful attempts to further her career. For both Joe and Marilyn, this imbalance brought them to a difficult place in their own lives, and near disaster in their careers. Fortunately they both had the kind of astuteness and even humility that once they realised what was happening, they set to and re-evaluated their situation, ending up with choices of behaviour that matched their own natures more fully.

Thinking about whether and how to change felt quite risky for each of them, because they felt that their organisation would not appreciate them changing, even though it was the organisation or colleagues who had let them know that what they were doing was not working sensibly. Each of them looked for some external support in thinking through where they were, what they wanted to achieve, how they wanted to "be" in the phase of their life that was starting now. Each then began to change slightly, adding in the kind of thinking and behaviour that was in fact quite natural to them, and therefore basically easy, but that they had not been using at work. As a result, they each not only became more effective, but also less dependent on being successful at work, feeling that this was how they wanted to be, even though it might have been career-limiting. Paradoxically, they both succeeded in career terms as well as feeling more content with themselves.

You cannot win them all

You've got to know when to hold
You've got to know when to fold,
You've got to know when to walk away,
You've got to know when to run. (*The gambler's song*)

One of the key skills or ways of thinking in exerting influence over others is that of being selective. This means choosing where and how you want to have an effect, and what the effect is that you want. This is the opposite of the need to get your own way all the time, which comes across more as a neurotic tendency than an ability to influence. The familiar 80/20 proportion can be used here, to remind us that in about 80 per cent of situations or decisions it does not matter very much who decides or what the decision is, within realistic limits. In 20 per cent it is critically important; and this is where to put your energy. In the 80 per cent abandon your pride, learn to feel comfortable with other people's actions and point of view. In the 20 per cent, bring all your skill, intuition and integrity to the situation, and in half of them, expect to have a result. In the remainder, it is probably not possible for you to affect or even reach the person with the most power in the situation.

How do you choose which are the important situations? I am reminded of a joke. A man is talking to someone on a train about his marriage: "We have the secret of a happy marriage" he says to his travel companion "I make only the important decisions, and my wife makes all the others." "That's interesting" is the reply, "who decides which are the important decisions?" "Oh," confidently, "my wife does that."

Time spent deciding on the important issues is essential. Revisiting your priorities, your values, your attitude to how you spend your time and energy is necessary. Using the decision tree method outlined in Chapter 3 may be of help in deciding which decisions you particularly want to influence. Using a relationship flow-chart may help you to decide which people you most need to influence. This is similar to the critical path described in Chapter 2, but highlights the people involved. It is a matter of reviewing and deciding which person has most power to affect your progress, your effectiveness or your contentment; and then finding a way to influence them appropriately.

Mapping out your relationships

4.1 Making and enriching the map to improve your understanding

Map out your relationship at work; include all the people with whom you need to relate to get the work done. Then widen the map to include people outside work. You may find that in different settings you use different styles which would transfer over well, once you realise the range of styles you have available. Diagram 4.1 is an example – Janet's map. Janet works in a small consultancy organisation and is part of a philosophy study group outside work.

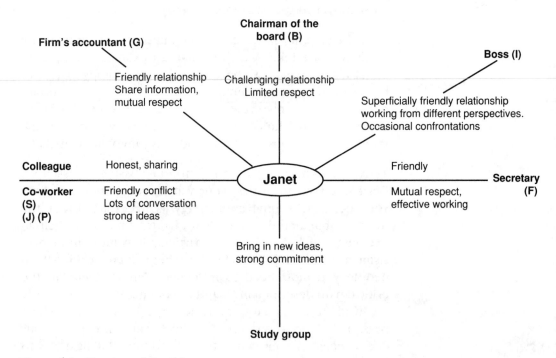

Figure 4.1   Mapping relationships

As Janet began to draw her map of the people who she wanted to influence and who influenced her, she noticed that she was most influential when with people at the same level as her, whom she respected, and particularly when she felt strongly about something. She realised she was less effective at influencing upwards. As she thought about this she realised that this was partly because of her own reaction to people in positions of authority which led her to behave in a less convincing way. She also realised that she was not clear about the amount of influence she had on people, and decided to chat informally to some colleagues to get a clearer picture.

When she considered her style, she noticed that "friendly" came up very often in the way she described her relationships. This led her to wonder whether she should sometimes pay more attention to stating her case clearly, and less to worrying about seeming friendly.

Joe (mentioned earlier in the chapter) did a similar mapping. He said that he had found a great difference between his style inside work which was consistently tough and abrasive and occasionally aggressive, and his social style where he was friendly, reliable and funny. On reflection he had realised that he had quite a strong influence on his group of friends, not through toughness but through trust and humour. This made him wonder about bringing some of his social style into work.

4.2 Setting yourself a framework

Consider who you need to influence and about what, in order to make an effective contribution to the direction of the organisation you are involved in. The following activity may help.

Step 1   *List the people you currently need to be able to carry out your work effectively.*

INFLUENCING WITHOUT AUTHORITY

Step 2   *For each one, consider their point of view. How do they see you? How do you think they react to you? Try stepping into their shoes as they meet with you – who do they see? What do they typically hear you say? What do **they** want from **you?** Reflect more deeply on what it is like to be them, their hopes, fears and ambitions.*

Step 3   *Give yourself some advice about how to deal with them in ways that respect their points of view, and makes the relationship easier and more effective.*

Result   *Once you let yourself pay attention to the information you already have (as in Step 2) it is not difficult to find ways of improving a working relationship.*

Developmental working relationships

You may be seen as manipulating or game-playing if you appear only to nurture relationships with people that can be useful to you. Looking at it another way, you can save yourself energy by making the assumption that all your relationships can be developmental. This is discussed usefully in a booklet published by the *Harvard Business Press* "Beyond the myth of the perfect mentor". This means making the assumption that all your working relationships can be mutually beneficial in some way and that you can *always* learn from them.

activity

4.3

This activity gives you the opportunity to consider what would happen if you were to reframe your goals and behaviour against a different set of criteria.

Step 1 Imagine that you have new targets which will be rewarded. The targets are these:

1. Over the next six months there will be a noticeable improvement, however slight, in 80 per cent of your working relationships in terms of courtesy, comfort and increased understanding.
2. You will have learned something that is of benefit to you from 70 per cent of the people you work with.
3. You will have improved your skills in eliciting and understanding the other person's perspective by 20 per cent – that is, for example, in one out of every five encounters you will have found out and understood something more of how they see the world and their values.
4. You will be able in 50 per cent of your serious encounters (meetings, appraisals, etc.) to explain your position in such a way that the other person understands it fully and can explain it back to you.

Step 2 Spend some moments reflecting seriously on what you would have to do and think so as to achieve these targets.

Step 3 Notice how you react to this idea.

Step 4 Write down your reactions, and read through what you have written. Be aware of the kind of language you are using, and reflect on any blocks you have to the notion of these imaginary targets. Some of these blocks may in fact be affecting your ability to influence people.

Result Linking your wish to meet targets to an aspect of life that is not generally described in this way gives you valuable insights not only into steps you can take, but also your own attitudes and possible blockages.

Choosing allies and champions

"Who cares? Who can? Who will?" There is plenty written elsewhere about delegation as a key to reducing workload and increasing opportunities for staff. In a pressured work situation people are tempted to delegate too much to already overloaded staff, who may themselves have no one to delegate on to. Alternatively, they do not delegate enough, either out of compassion for their staff, or out of habits of holding on and mistrust of others. (There is more about delegation in Chapter 6.)

Let us look at it a new way. Delegation implies a top-down process, a kind of sieving, where we shed jobs and responsibilities, holding on to some, and letting others "downwards" in a scale of decreasing importance. In another way of looking at it, you can imagine a process of equal sharing, in all directions, according to what people can do, want to do, and are interested in doing. Some project teams and matrix management groups work like this, and the principle can be applied in all kinds of situations, even hierarchical ones. It means taking a more pragmatic and less dramatic approach to work, and being able to understand the interests and motivations of people around you. If you consider jobs to be done or information to be collected in a reality based way rather than a catastrophic one (which means watching your thinking patterns as described in Chapter 1) it is usually possible to sort them, and match them to the most likely people in terms of their interest and ability to do them, including your colleagues and your boss or others senior to you. It means looking at your organisation as a system rather than as a pyramid. (There is more about this approach in Chapter 9.) There are very many tasks or responsibilities which are hard or demanding for you, but easy and interesting for someone else; find those other people.

I worked once with a small voluntary organisation, where the project leader and her colleagues never managed to keep the filing up to date, partly because they had other things to do and partly because they hated filing. Not doing it also demoralised them. A suggestion was made "Find someone who likes filing as a volunteer". When they had got over their disbelief that such a person existed, they found a volunteer who did indeed enjoy filing. The filing was not done perfectly, but at least it was done; and the team were energised by the change in pattern from being stuck with a looming pile of filing waiting to be done which they were not doing, to looking at ways of improving it to help the volunteer.

Negotiating as a form of influence

Negotiation is a basic means of getting what you want from others. It is a back-and-forth communication designed to reach an agreement when you and the other side have some interests which are shared and some which are opposed. (Fisher and Ury, 1997)

As Fisher and Ury go on to say, standard strategies for negotiation often leave people worn out or alienated. They have some suggestions for a less exhausting and destructive approach which they call "Principled Negotiation" (where one of their attractive quotes is "be hard on the merits, soft on the people") and avoiding taking a position that you then have to defend. In defending our position, they suggest, we can unwittingly trap ourselves into having our pride or our ego locked into defending the position for its own sake, rather than for its merits, which may mean that the basic need in successful negotiation – to meet the underlying concerns of both parties – is overlooked. For this reason they advise us to separate the people from the problem, and to focus on the interests of each party rather than their positions. Searching for criteria, externally focused, that would define a fair solution helps us let go of the worry about seeming to "give in".

Fisher and Ury have interesting suggestions about dealing with the situation when the person we are negotiating with has more power, where the odds are stacked against us. They recommend two points – be sure to protect yourself against making an agreement you should reject, and be sure to make the most of what you do have in your favour. One way of approaching this is to look at what the alternatives are to reaching a negotiated solution – remembering that the only reason for negotiation is to get something better than what we would get without the effort of negotiating. It is important, therefore, to be very clear about what to do if it is impossible to come to an agreement with the other party. This needs to be clarified because otherwise the thought of it remains as an unexplored "threat" that drives us into an emotional form of negotiation that weakens our case, clouds our thinking and uses unnecessary energy. The rational emotive approach outlined in Chapter 1 can help with managing our reactions to unexplored emotional threats.

As well as this, having a clear picture of what we can do if the negotiating does not work gives us more power in the negotiating position. As Fisher, Ury and Patton suggest, the better our alternative the better our power in the negotiating position. I have seen this approach in action, as have most people, in many settings. It transforms negotiation from an obsolete form of struggle into an elegant example of professional skill built on integrity.

Matching, pacing and leading

In the area of sales training a lot of work has been done in noticing how effective salespeople work. The same principles can be used in convincing people about your ideas or to see things your way, and to help you connect with their experience.

4.4

If you are not already familiar with this approach, you may want to try it out.

The first step is to match yourself to the other person's position, in terms of how they are sitting, breathing, moving. This is equivalent symbolically to moving your position from sitting opposite to them to sitting beside them so that you can see what they are looking at. It is a way of aligning yourself to a certain degree to their point of view; this makes it more possible for them to see your point of view too. It does not mean imitating them, but in some way echoing their movements and posture with your own.

Begin to match yourself, lightly, to the kind of language they are using. If their language and motivation is about money and markets, do not begin your conversation about feelings, and vice versa. In the same way that it is a courtesy to attempt to speak a little in the national language of a person you are working with, people find it encouraging if you talk their topic or metaphor language too, but in a small way – do not overdo it. As well as making them feel more comfortable, you will also find that attempting to frame your ideas in another person's style of talking increases your understanding of where you may have some common ground.

Once you have begun to match, you then "pace", which is the same as running alongside them if you were an athlete. In this case we are talking about style of language, both words and body language. Then, following your instinct, you move into "leading", where you are introducing something new from your perspective. If you have carried this through and maintained respect for the other person, you will find that they begin to see your point of view in a way that can be integrated with their own.

Because this style builds trust, it is really important to be genuine about it. The "let down" that people feel if you prove untrustworthy, will cancel any gains.

Using conflict creatively

Do you feel that the ideas so far would take all the fun out of a good fight? Many people are most able to be convinced of a new point of view by real conflict, "thrashing it out". They have a heated argument, then go away and think it over, ending up with seeing the alternative point of view. This too is highly effective, among people who enjoy this style. It has an open and honest feel, and is sometimes part of a strong developmental relationship. This works best when there is a secure level of trust and an implicit agreement that this is meant to be a constructive rather than destructive process. In the UK and the USA, this style can be seen most frequently among men, particularly men in their twenties and thirties It may be more widespread as an acceptable style in Latin or Hispanic countries than in northern European ones.

Conflict

Although we have different ways of understanding, valuing and handling it, conflict is natural in all groups in human society. Strengthening your ability to value and transform conflict enriches your influencing skills, and saves you using up energy in fruitless or unresolved differences and battles. It is not necessarily problematic, as we can see from the paragraph above. It is however most seriously problematic when the conflict is not resolved. Unresolved conflict leads to destructive outcomes. At one extreme we have the blood feud or vendetta, a continuing series of "revenges", where the last offence is seen as payment for the previous one, but which itself leads to a further retribution. At the other extreme, the more private one, unresolved conflict leads to stress, hidden anger and even illness. A healthy organisation, a healthy person and a healthy society all have acceptable ways of acknowledging conflict, and as far as possible surfacing and resolving it.

Why do conflicts arise?

One of the most frequent causes of conflict in organisational or family life is difference in personality type that is not understood or valued. These differences often mean that people are working from assumptions that they believe are universally held, but which in fact are particular to their personality type. As well as this, conflict is caused by differences of will, where individuals have a continual personal need to get their own way; and getting their own way is more important, at the moment of conflict, than anything else. Conflict is very often seen at the moments when different sets of assumptions or values come up against each other, when both parties genuinely think they are right at a deep level. Other grounds for conflict include battles over power, over allocation of resources, over different goals or purposes, or different ways of doing things.

4.5 Your own patterns about conflict

Step 1 *Reflect for a moment on how you yourself react to not getting your own way, to having to go along with other people's ideas when you do not agree with them.*

Step 2 *Notice how you react to people who have very different values from your own, values that you do not agree with or that you may even find offensive. Can you work with such people? How do you manage disagreements with them? Where are the main sources of conflict?*

Step 3 *Recall a conflict that you did resolve, and one that stayed unresolved. Find ways of noticing the differences between the two examples: how they started, how they progressed and what you feel or remember about them now.*

Step 4 *Recall a time when you were, or thought yourself to be, in competition with someone. How did the situation affect you? What kind of behaviour did it trigger on your part? What might have been the alternatives?*

Result *Influencing without authority needs a sophisticated approach to managing conflict, so that you do not find yourself using time or energy inappropriately, in going over old confrontations, planning revenge, building up your emotional reaction. Understanding your own basic approach is a first step in building your skills and influence. The Table overleaf may help you understand your patterns.*

INFLUENCING WITHOUT AUTHORITY

Table 4.1 Approaches to conflict

Do you prefer to collaborate?
Useful when:

- both sets of concerns are too important to be compromised, and you need to include both
- you need to learn by understanding the views of others
- people have different perspectives on a problem that are all valuable
- you need to work through hard feelings which have been interfering with an interpersonal relationship
- you want to gain commitment to a group decision.

Do you prefer to compete?
Useful when:

- quick decisive action is vital
- when you know you are right and other people's welfare is at stake
- you are dealing with people who will take advantage of non-competitive behaviour.

Do you often avoid conflict and keep out of the way?
Useful when:

- other more important issues are pressing
- you see no chance of satisfying your concerns
- the potential damage of confronting a conflict outweighs the benefits
- people need to cool down to regain perspective and composure
- the need for information-gathering outweighs the advantages of an immediate decision
- others can resolve the conflict more effectively
- the issue is only symptomatic of a more basic issue.

Do you prefer to accommodate or "give in"?
Useful when:

- you realise you are wrong
- the issue is much more important to the other person than to you
- continued competition would only damage your cause
- avoiding disruption is especially important
- allowing others to experiment and learn from their mistakes.

Do you prefer to compromise?
Useful when:

- goals are moderately important but not worth the effort of potential disruption of more assertive approaches
- two opponents with equal power are strongly committed to mutually exclusive goals
- trying to achieve temporary settlements to complex issues
- expedient solutions are needed in a short time
- collaborations or competition fails.

Benefits of acknowledging conflict and managing it well

You will probably have some experience of the benefits of well-resolved conflict. You may have noticed how work relationships and private ones, too, can be strengthened as a result of working openly through differences, even though this can feel risky. You may have found that you trust people more after a clearly resolved conflict.

Coming through a conflict effectively and humanely is likely to build your value for yourself, your self-esteem. I have had the feeling in a conflict where I have stayed with my feet on the ground, of suddenly knowing where I stood and feeling secure and grounded in that.

You will probably have noticed as well that conflict, effectively managed, is a frequent factor in creativity and that active discussion between people with differing interests or opinions can lead to increased productivity.

Because conflict is a real and human thing, a job where you are expected to work through differences productively carries a fuller meaning and, therefore, more satisfaction with the job itself.

Clearly, positive effects like this are only likely if conflict is managed constructively. The nature of conflicts and their resolution will also be influenced by our general pattern of relationships at work and our perception and interpretation of conflict-related events. The key steps in managing conflict are:

1. Acknowledging the differences.
2. Seeing differences as valuable rather than problematic.
3. Keeping the common goal in sight at all times.
4. Set up ground-rules about how to disagree.
5. Plan for divergent discussions for alternatives, as well as convergent discussions to choose options and plan.
6. Take out the "personal" element and focus on the contribution.

A person who can help to manage conflict creatively develops a high level of informal influence, respect and personal authority.

INFLUENCING WITHOUT AUTHORITY

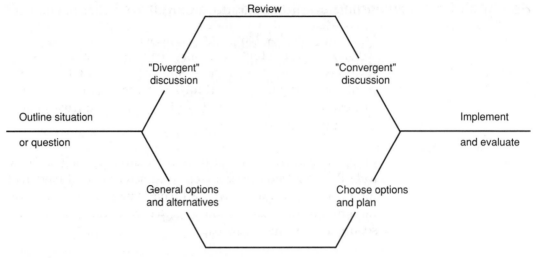

Figure 4.2 Managing difference in the decision-making process

Marshall Rosenberg and non-violent communication

I myself am very attracted by Rosenberg's model of communication that he uses and teaches in the mediation and resolution of conflict. As he says:

the central intention behind the process is to get to a place where people can respond to one another out of compassion; where they clearly understand what each other's needs are, and are able to communicate about them in a way that makes it comfortable for others to respond to these needs (Marshall Rosenberg in an interview on the Internet)

As he says, when we are not getting our needs met, we tend to think in terms of what is wrong with the other person; we have an intellectual way of analysing people and classifying them into good and bad, right and wrong. He sees a more effective way where we use a language that comes from the heart rather than from the head, describing our own wishes without criticising or judging the other person. When working with a conflict, he prefers to use phrases such as "what is it that you would like from one another, to resolve the differences that exist and are creating violence or conflict between you". The key, he suggests, is to shift from making judgements of each other into finding what each person or group wants from the other. Most of us find that really difficult. It is certainly worth working at.

Interestingly when people at first get in touch with what they actually want, it is either very vague, not possible to get, or not really what they would appreciate if they got it. Following through the discussion or thought process to clarity is an essential aspect of Rosenberg's approach. His belief is that we can develop the ability to hear the request behind the message, however aggressively the message is conveyed. It is also necessary to learn not to get into the business of evaluating whether we agree with the wish expressed behind the outward message or whether, indeed, we can do anything about it. What is important is to connect with the person and show that you have accurately understood, before worrying about whether you can do anything about it. We need to be aware all the time that the person we are speaking with may be operating under a whole different language system than we are, which can lead to misunderstandings. We need to find ways of staying within our system of looking for what the other person needs, regardless of how the other person communicates. We also need to be able to make a gap, a distance, between hearing and understanding what the other person wants, and the feeling that if we know what they want, we will be obliged to make it happen. This is often what blocks us from allowing ourselves to hear what they want.

Managing meetings with influence

Most of the people I have worked with, particularly in organisations going through change, complain that their working days are bedevilled by meetings that seem to them to be pointless or time-wasting. Their main question seems to be: "How can I make the meetings shorter, less frequent or more valuable." Paradoxically, people who complain about meetings do not do very much to change the situation when they themselves are in meetings. If this is an issue for you, there are several aspects you should be paying attention to.

Attendance versus non-attendance – should I go?

Review the short-term and long-term effects of going and not going. Who will notice? How will it affect your position? Will you miss any essential information and, if so, how else will you obtain it if you do not go? If the meeting is not genuinely going to be valuable to you, it is better not to go, unless that will damage you politically. If that is the case, and you feel you must be at a meeting, however unwillingly, be sure to get some value for yourself out of the meeting. I have seen people turning up "because you have to" and then sitting resentfully and silently all through the meeting. This does not enhance their reputation or people's respect for them. Other people I have seen use the time (even when the meeting itself has not been of much importance to them, and they were there "because they had to be") to make alliances, exchange information on the network, or to have some reflection time. This seems a more realistic approach.

If you are not chairing

- Influencing the agenda – who sets it? When? How are agenda items ordered? You may have options in influencing some of these. This means taking some time or making some effort beforehand, which will pay off in terms of having more useful time at the meeting.
- Influencing the time management of the meeting. Often, if already not willing to be at a meeting, we can ourselves get caught up in repetitive arguments, contributing to the time-wasting ourselves. It is helpful to use phrases, through the Chair if necessary, that can help move things on. These may include "What are we actually trying to decide here?", "What other information do we need?" "I wonder whether we are in a position to decide just now" "I would be interested to hear from X about their experience in this situation" "How did we deal with this before?"
- It is also helpful at the beginning wherever possible to set a time frame for yourself, and say at the outset how much time you have, and go at the time you have said that you will.
- Contributing effectively to the decision-making in the meeting. This can be done by bringing some attention and energy to bear, and using some of the phrases above. If you have a clear model in your mind of how decision-

making goes, you can keep track of the process and nudge it along.

- Maintain a cheerful approach, even if you are being challenging. In every case, if you are at a meeting, willingly or unwillingly, bringing a sanguine mood, a cheerful approach and an assumption (outwardly at least) that the meeting is meant to achieve something, is more effective than sitting in a rage of frustration. It will also usually help the meeting to be over more quickly.

If you are chairing

Review your own skills in chairing meetings. How do you rate on:

- making sure everyone has a hearing
- helping the dominators to avoid dominating
- clarifying which agenda items are for decisions, action, information, sharing or discussion
- keeping to time
- allocating time proportionate to the importance of the item.
- making time for breaks and thinking
- watching and managing the social process as well as the task process.

Be aware, if you are chairing, that if people have come, their participation is probably needed, and be sure that you encourage that to happen. Be clear what the meeting is intended to achieve that cannot be achieved any better way, and set your sights on achieving it. Check whether any of the purposes of the meeting could be achieved in other ways. Peter Honey (1997) has a useful workbook of questionnaires on chairing meetings.

Problems with influencing and ways of resolving them

Mind-reading

One of the ways I have noticed people sabotaging their own ability to be influential is by talking as if they can mind-read. They use phrases such as "I know why she's doing this, you know", or "He's only in it for the opportunity to sabotage me". Certainly they are sometimes right in guessing some of other people's range of intentions, but it is hard to be accurate about the sources of other people's actions, their real or deep intentions. If you find yourself doing this, it is probably more useful to:

- pay extra attention and increase your insight into your own motives
- "assume positive intent", that is, to look for the positive human motive behind the action
- try saying the same things or thinking the same thoughts about yourself: sometimes we see in others what is in fact true for us
- focus on what someone is actually doing, their behaviour and the effect of the behaviour, than to surmise about their motives.

"Giving away" your power

Many managers and employees attribute more power to the people senior to them than they actually have, and move themselves further and further into a victim position. If you find yourself doing this, it is probably important to:

- attend to your body language: your breathing, your posture, your expression and your voice. This has a positive inward effect as well as an outward one
- go through Activity 4.2 about someone senior to you
- be aware of your thought processes, using some of the attitudes in Chapter 1
- maintain a sense of balance and humour.

Being unclear about your priorities: giving mixed messages

People who are clear themselves and transparent with others about their values and priorities exert a great deal of influence, often unconsciously. People who are muddled and opaque themselves have more problems. If this is the case for you, you probably need to:

- review and sort your priorities and discuss them with someone else

- find ways of conveying those priorities to the people you need to influence, in language that makes sense to them
- make an effort to find out and discuss their priorities.

Trying to be liked rather than wanting to be respected

Some people very much want to be liked. They are afraid to state a different point of view or stand up to someone for fear of being rejected. If this is the case for you, you probably need to:

- practise stating your case in small, safe situations
- spend time in reflecting on what else you want as well as to be liked, and focus on that
- remind yourself that work is a place for work as much as for social relationships
- watch someone who is liked and is also assertive and is listened to. See what they do and talk to them.

Conclusion

Influencing effectively can help you survive. It can help you tune in to the "flows" of energy in the organisation and among the people around you. You can shift to a "minimalist" style of working, conserving energy by cooperation, by working alongside, by valuing and resolving conflict and by being clear about who to influence and connect with. To influence well you need to bring resolve and integrity to the situation, to be selective and to prioritise your energy in influencing. You also need to understand the micropolitics of the organisation; who has the power to make something change, and who might care enough to take action. Using your ability to influence informally, you will be able to help the organisation or group you are with to move in its chosen direction, using less time and energy, and with more satisfaction.

5 Managing with more differences and less problems

Introduction

- In a difficult or pressured work situation, you certainly do not have time for unnecessary and time-consuming misunderstandings. This chapter is designed to help you reduce some of the misunderstandings that arise from basic differences and the way we deal with diversity.

- We all have the dilemma that on the one hand we are more comfortable with "people of our own kind" some of the time, and yet find people who are "different" stimulating and interesting. As humans we seem to have difficulty valuing people who are different from us, and yet to like the idea of variety and uniqueness. We can waste time and energy in trying to make people the same as us or as some idealised norm, and we can lose good opportunities for using resources well by mis-understanding or misinterpreting what others are doing. In order to manage more with less, each of us needs to move forward in the way we understand and work with people who are different from us.

Attitudes to diversity

Much of the work on diversity originated from the fact that some groups in most or all societies are unfairly treated, stereotyped in a negative way and even persecuted. In Western society this includes women, people with disabilities, and minority religious or cultural groups. Even in the "micro" environment of our immediate group or work team, we still have the tendency to behave unfairly, in the sense of not valuing their contribution, to people who we perceive as being different from us or different from a "norm" that we have developed. This is partly a matter of power and control: people of the same sort are thought to be easier to control and motivate because "one package fits all" and no energy needs to be spent in considering the possible different ways of controlling, motivating and rewarding. Interestingly, though, however small and homogeneous a group is, each person will notice their own differences from the group and wish to be recognised as such in some small way.

More recently, a different approach has been taken, both in countries and in organisations. In this approach, the emphasis has not been on fairness or unfairness, but on richness and variety. In countries with a wide range of cultural groups which have begun to have a voice, politicians and others have realised the power of some of these subgroups, and also the loss to society of having groups of people who are disenfranchised, unemployed or in despair. Organisations that have "cloned" themselves, in that they have defined a narrow set of desired characteristics in the staff they employ, are not able to respond to new circumstances flexibly because the groups they employ have a narrow set of assumptions, behaviour and ways of thinking. Organisations that have looked for a wide variety of staff can be more responsive, because they have people with a wide range of behaviours and thinking. When new ways are required, there are people already inside the organisation for whom it is not new, who can respond quickly and who can introduce others easily to the new requirements.

As well as this, with the internationalisation and globalisation of business, we are having to meet, work with, do business and negotiate with people from very different worlds, who are by no means a minority and who need to be dealt with differently. It was interesting to note the sudden increase in interest in cross-cultural management when Japan and other countries on the Pacific rim began to be seen as significant world players in business. Americans and British in particular were forced to realise that the "Do it our way or no deal" approach was losing them business. To take a cynical view, when "foreigners" were less powerful, businesspeople saw no need to learn their ways. When the power balance changed, so did attitudes about diversity.

As managers and as private individuals, it is likely that we will be meeting and working with a wider and wider set of people with different habits, different belief systems about work and different ways of relating. To be effective we need to be aware of these differences, work flexibly and respectfully with them, while maintaining a sense of our own values and identity.

Using this chapter

The chapter covers a variety of ways of looking at diversity and difference. The overall purpose of the chapter is to provide tools, techniques and ways of thinking that help you manage your own approach to how you cope with difference, differences within your team such as motivation and personality type, potential differences between men and women at home and at work, and other differences that can lead to misunderstanding.

Most people reading this book will have already worked out, in the process of their everyday lives, some strategies for working effectively with people who are different from them. The chapter is designed to remind you of things you already know and strategies you use, and to add new frameworks and techniques.

The differences that make a difference

If you find you are spending what seem like inappropriate amounts of time and energy in trying to convince people, in repeating yourself, in putting things right that should be done well routinely in your opinion, check whether some of the difficulties are due to unexplored basic differences. These differences are likely to be about ways of thinking, about personality type, about action and learning preferences, about basic motivations, about priorities and about choice of language.

Cross-cultural working: more with less

Some of the most difficult differences to cope with or even recognise are the deep cultural assumptions that individuals, groups and nations may have. They tend to be about five aspects of human life, which may be called cultural dilemmas. Different cultures, as Fons Trompenaars (1993) suggests, solve these dilemmas by choosing one answer or one end of a continuum which then becomes institutionalised as "right".

The everlasting questions or dilemmas he identifies can be as described below:

1. Is a person responsible primarily to themselves for their own life as an individual, or is a person primarily responsible to their group or community? If there was a conflict between the individual's own good and the good of the group or community, which should a person put first? (*Dilemma*: individual or community first?)
2. Where should we put our loyalty? If we had to choose, is it better to be loyal to a universal principle or ideal such as morality, the law or the state, or to be loyal to one's friends and family? (*Dilemma*: choosing according to general principles, or particular situations?)
3. To what extent, and how, should we express our emotions? How do we decide how much of our feelings to show? (*Dilemma*: which is appropriate – control your emotions or express them freely?)
4. How do we manage our personal privacy, and the different aspects of our lives? (*Dilemma*: be specific about who we let in, and to what areas; or once a person is close to us, they have access to everything?)
5. How do you evaluate a person? What makes a person worthy of respect or interest? Do we pay most attention to what they are doing now, or their background, experience, family?) (*Dilemma*: judge a person by what they do and achieve, or who they are and what they represent?)
6. To what extent are we in charge of our own fate and destiny, and controllers of our environment? (*Dilemma*: can we control the forces of nature, or do they control us?)

When I have discussed this issue with groups of managers, asking them to place themselves somewhere on the continuum represented by each of the above six questions, I have noticed that people can locate themselves personally, as they experience the world, and they can also generalise about their own group or nationality.

What is important, in terms of managing more with less, is to be aware of these basic differences in assumptions, and understand how they may lead to difficulties for those who believe that their answer to any one of the questions is *the* answer, rather than *an* answer.

Let us look further at some of the differences, and how they may affect everyday working life. For example, if you are working with a mixed group, some of whom have an individualistic set of assumptions, and some a more collective set, how will the reward system work? Will you have individual bonuses, or work group bonuses? How much time will you spend in fruitless argument about it, without understanding where the real disagreement comes from? If there are differences in values about how you assess the worth of a person, what will you do about target-setting and promotion? Will you rely only on the last month's or quarter's results, or will you include longer-term achievements, education, contribution to the general culture? To manage more and different people, these differences need to be taken into account. The secret is in refraining from an "either/or" mode and looking for a "both/and" solution, if you want to get the best commitment from a group of people who are working from very different assumptions.

A further difference that causes many problems between people is seen in our attitudes to time; to deadlines, to ways of organising our day, to "punctuality". Some of this is referred to in Chapter 6.

Understanding and managing cross-cultural differences are covered more fully in Trompenaars's book mentioned above, and also by John Mole (1995) in *Mind your Manners*. Not all differences are cross-cultural, however. Differences in assumptions can also be seen within groups, between men and women, and between disciplines or departments. Try out the six questions for yourself, with people you know or with your own work group. Notice how tempted some people are to argue about the rights and wrongs of the dilemmas, rather than to notice the many different ways of looking at the world.

5.1

Table 5.1 contains a simple set of questions which introduce the five cultural dilemmas outlined by Trompenaars. Locate yourself at a point along each continuum. It is important to be aware of two things: first, that there are no right and wrongs here, only different positions or ways of viewing the world; and second, that we are very inclined to believe that our way, our position on the continuum, is the right one. We can see the faults or problems in other points of view, but find it hard to see what might be problematic with our own.

Table 5.1 Cultural assumptions: what is your position?

1. Is a person mainly responsible for themselves and their own life as an individual, or is a person primarily part of a group or community?

   Individual ——————————————————— Collective/community

2. Which is more important and worthy: loyalty to particular friends for family, or loyalty to something greater such as the law, morality, the organisation or the State?

   Universal (to the law, organisation etc.) ——— Particular (to family and friends etc.)

3. What is the appropriate way to express emotions?

   Neutral (controlled expression) ————— Affective (expressive show of feeling)

4. How do we manage our area of privacy: who do we let in, when and why?

   Specific ———————————————————— Diffuse
   (let people into specific areas for   (once in, a person has access
   specific purposes only)   to all areas)

5. How do you estimate the worth of an individual or group?

   Achieving ——————————————————— Ascribing
   (by what you can see them do)   (events are controlled by external forces)

6. How much control do we have over what happens to us?

   Internal ———————————————————— External
   (events are controlled by my efforts)   (events are controlled by external forces)

Where would you put (a) yourself, (b) your own nationality in general and (c) where would you put your organisation?

Different personality types

Another way of describing the ways in which people differ stems from Jung's concept of introvert and extrovert. In this way of understanding, people differ in the way they view the world in basic ways. "Introverts" are particularly interested, and motivated by, such things as achievement, fulfilment, tasks, knowledge and understanding, and fantasy, with their interest directed primarily inward and then secondarily outward. People with an "extrovert" tendency on the other hand are more noticeably interested in status and respect, with their interest directed primarily outward to people, action, domination and facts, and only secondarily inwards.

Jung's ideas were taken forward by Isobel Myers and Katherine Briggs (1962) into a personality type questionnaire which many people are familiar with. This way of categorising people can be very useful in helping people to come to terms with the inherent normal differences between people; at the same time such a typology runs the risk that in its own way it also stereotypes people, even though it is designed to increase understanding.

An earlier typology matches the Myers–Briggs type indicator (MBTI) quite comfortably, drawing on the ancient Greek "temperaments" – "Dionysian", "Epimethean", "Promethean" and "Apollonian" – suggesting that each of them focuses primarily on one of four underlying motivations – freedom to act, social status, power, or self-actualisation – which are also linked with joy and release, duty, science and knowledge, and spirit (Kiersey and Bates, 1984). How would you typify yourself?

As with cultural assumptions, our tendency is to believe that our inclination or temperament is the only one and also the right one, which leads us to misunderstand others and their motives. Looking at these different types of typology can be used to widen our appreciation of the richness and variety of the human personality, and the wide range of assumptions and behaviours available to social groups. Some people find it very useful to explore their own "type" and get a clearer understanding of how it compares to other "types", using the "MBTI" questionnaire. This is best done with someone who understands the richness of the data it generates and has the skills to interpret the implications. This process can also give you some real insights into ways of engaging effectively with people who are a different "type".

Problems of diversity

As mentioned in the introduction, our tendency is often to prefer or feel more comfortable with people like ourselves, and stereotype or reject people who are different. Why is this? One reason is that of discomfort. Being with other people who see the world differently can be challenging to our own assumptions and even to our identity. If I value myself for a certain reason, for instance my ability to achieve results or my good education, and I spend time with people who genuinely see no value in that, I have a problem. I may feel that they do not value me. They may in fact value me highly, but for their own reasons not mine.

I may also feel affronted when I see that they do not think well of the things I admire. As well as this, we must remember that the people that we see as "different" or "difficult" may also see us in the same way, which may add to the discomfort of both.

activity

5.2

This is a development of Activity 5.1, taking you deeper into an understanding of different cultural assumptions. There are five pairs of statements below, describing differing personal viewpoints, putting the deeper reasons for those viewpoints.

Step 1   *Read through the statements. For each pair, notice which most corresponds to your own view, and to what extent you can appreciate the alternative.*

Step 2   *See whether you can match any of the views to people you know.*

Step 3   *Imagine how a person from each point of view would react to you as a colleague, based on what you know about yourself and how you behave.*

1. *"Some people I naturally admire. They have a kind of presence; people seem to be drawn to them. They know how to behave. This is often because they come from a family that is like that, which people look up to because of their history; through several generations they have lived valuable lives. That makes a lot of difference to me. It seems to help a person to live a good life if they have had a good background. Even a really good company can help a person in that way; I like to meet people who have worked in organisations that have made a real contribution to the world. I like to show respect to people with wisdom and experience from the life they have lived. It makes a more orderly world.*

   I notice that the best leaders often come from schools or families where there are other good leaders or people who have done well in some way. I'm not saying that you can't improve yourself by your own efforts – I've met people who have come from nothing and have really made good. But it's more of an effort for them: and it doesn't always last. You can see that by what happens to their children. I've seen people, too, from good backgrounds who disgraced themselves; but they stand out because they're the exception.

   People that have got somewhere entirely by their own efforts seem very preoccupied with what they do all the time. To me, it's not only about what you do, it's where you fit in. You are what you are, even if you don't get things done. Who wants a world full of frantic achievers all proving how good they are by what they do? There's more to life than that. I don't think people should be given a lot of status and power just because they're great achievers; it's the kind of person you are and your way of thinking that matters too. After all, it's not easy to manage power well."

2. *"The people I admire are people who have made something of themselves. I'm not interested in their background or upbringing; my question is 'What are they contributing?' A person at the top needs to show that they can do the job better, work harder, or bring something special.*

   I like to believe in a world where we all start equal: you shouldn't have special advantages because of your family or school. I think people should earn their status, and keep on doing better if they want to keep it. It may sound tough but a person to me is as good as their last results.

   *I don't like to see royalty and people like that getting special treatment. I'm as good as the next person, in my opinion, and I don't respect someone just because they're older or more senior. What have they **done** is always my question."*

3. *"I don't believe in slopping your feelings all over the place. Emotions have got nothing to do with the outside world; they belong to oneself. I have very strong feelings; but that's my business. I find it very unprofessional when people can't keep their feelings to themselves; feelings that get the better of you can twist judgements.*

   Some people I know are like a bunch of children: highs and lows, shaking your hand, leaning close; really quite embarrassing to see such a public display of what should be kept to one's own private circle. They also seem to need to prove that they are feeling what they're feeling in such an obvious way. There seems to be no room for subtlety, or even for different grades of emotion. It's all or nothing with them.

If I were upset about something, for instance when I'm travelling, I wouldn't expect to have to make a song and dance about it before something was done. I would expect things to be put right because they were wrong, not because I felt one way or the other about it. If I am upset and things aren't improved, I don't use that service again if I have any choice. I don't like a lot of fuss; I like to see people with self-respect and a sense of dignity and calm, behaving in a businesslike and professional manner. That's what impresses me."

4. *"I naturally show how I feel. The feeling is there and why hide it? I like to see what other people are feeling too. It surprises me how some people don't seem to feel anything; same face, same tone of voice whatever happens. It seems a bit inhuman to me. Or even if they are angry or even happy, you would never know it. I can't imagine what it would be to live in a world where everyone was like that. I sometimes think they must be ashamed of their emotions; they certainly look embarrassed when you greet them normally or react to what they're saying.*

   I know some people who'll take any kind of insult and not look at you, not react. Either they're emotionally dead, or else they're deceitful; I haven't worked out which. In any case it seems very odd. I often wonder if they're plotting revenge! In fact, it always shows in the end if a person is upset, so they might as well show it in the first place. I believe in honesty, at work and at home. Not showing your feelings is a form of dishonesty to me. They may think they're being "rational", but I don't agree, abnormal is what it is to me. The same with pleasure and delight; I like people to know when I'm pleased, and I like to know if they're pleased too. Why hide it, it's a part of real life".

5. *"I'm a person who likes to weigh people up before deciding if I want to know them. After all, once you get to know a person, you're an open book. You don't want just anyone in your life. I prefer to do business with people that fit into my scheme of things, see life in some similar kind of way, know the proper ways to behave.*

I don't care to do business with people until I know them quite well, see if they can be trusted. I sometimes find that you can tell a lot about a person's style of doing business by finding out what they think about politics, art and so on. How they treat their family is another thing that matters to me. After all, you can't divide your life up into compartments can you: you're the same person wherever you are.

The people I do business with can get very close to me. Some families we've known for years. Many of my employees and colleagues have asked me to be their children's godfather. We go to their weddings, worry about their divorces. It can be a real community. Many of our employees go on holiday together.

When I travel on business, I find it odd the way some people seem to want to get to know me in a hurry, ask rather nosy questions. What's the hurry? Real relationships, whether they start as work or as friendship, take time."

6. *"I'm a person who believes you should keep work and private life apart. Yes I'll talk about my family, doesn't everybody; but you've got to suit what you do to the circumstances. I like to be friendly to everyone; we're a big happy family where I work; but that doesn't mean we're lifelong friends for instance. Mind you, we get on well, first name terms quite a lot of the time. Even our*

MD, Dr Antony Levenson, at work or officially is Tony when we're not being formal.

I'm my own person; what you see is what you get. I'll talk to anyone; I don't like these reserved people that seem to be judging you before they'll even say hello. I like to be conversational, find out what business people are in and so on. That's the way to get on with people in my opinion, in a general way. I'd say I was a quick judge of character, at least from a business point of view.

Close friends? Oh that's a different thing altogether. Like I said, there are some things you keep to yourself. I know some great people at work; but if I moved jobs I don't know that I'd keep up with them.

Travelling I like to get to know people a bit; well it's interesting to meet people, that's what travel is for. And you're never going to meet them again after all."

7. *"People like us believe that we should look after each other to get the best out of life. After all, we're social animals, and that's how we operate best. We're in this world to make the best of this life, so let's use the talents of everyone to make things work.*

Our best achievements, if you look around, are never done alone: there's always a group somewhere. Even effective leaders need a good band of followers. On holiday too you can see it; look how much fun people have when they're with their family or a group of friends.

I always feel really sorry for people who have to travel by themselves. Seeing businessmen all by themselves on a train you have to wonder why they don't have anyone to travel with them and help them. We would never expect one of our people to travel and do business by themselves; it wouldn't make any sense at all.

Sometimes it would be nice to do things a bit more in my own way, I suppose; but that's only in the short term. Long term, it makes so much more sense to work as a group. That's what I say to my children when they want to do things their own way, without taking into account the rest of the family. How would we be able to look out for each other and help each other to lead the life we each really want, if we had to do it all alone all the time? How do you get the best life for yourself, if you have to do it in a vacuum? Take account of the organisation that matters to you, and then the organisation will be in good shape to take account of you."

8. *"I am a person who believes that individual freedom is very important, and that is the route to a good quality of life for everyone. People should start by developing their own strengths so that they can stand on their own feet. The more a person can manage by themselves, the more I admire them.*

I always prefer to travel alone, so that I don't have to keep on checking what other people are wanting. I prefer to make my own decisions and act on them. I'm known as a decisive person.

I have always believed that a person has to make what they can out of their own life; if everyone is responsible for themselves, we will have a better society. I don't believe in this collective stuff. Obviously if someone has a disaster, they may need a helping hand to get them back on their feet again; but then they should be able to get on with their lives."

9. *"I am a person who believes that there are universal truths about right and wrong and you have to stick to those. You can tell a good person by the sacrifices they will make if asked, when there is a moral issue. The law has to be above personal or friendship considerations, otherwise where would we all be?*

I would trust a person if I thought they would stick to their word through thick and thin, even if the circumstances change. A rule is a rule, in my book. Yes obviously people matter, but what kind of world would we live in if everything had to be decided on individually? It would be chaos. You've got to have agreed rules, laws, contracts which you can expect people to stick to, whatever particular circumstances are."

10. *"I am a person who believes that loyalty to my friends is the most important way of showing that I am a good person.*

Rules and the law are obviously important in a general way, but they should never be used in an impersonal or objective way: individual people come first.

I would trust a person who honours the fact that circumstances can change. There are usually several ways of looking at a situation, and who can tell which is the right one?

I couldn't trust a person who would let down a friend or his family, just for some kind of rule or contract. What kind of a person would do that?

The one thing you can be sure of in this life is that the people around you matter. You are lucky if you have real friends and family, and so it makes sense to put them first.

If I had to choose between breaking a law and protecting my family or a friend, of course I would put the people I care about first. What else would you expect a decent person to do?"

Result   *This gives you the opportunity to "step into someone else's shoes". The activity can increase the depth of your understanding, and ability to respond effectively to people with a different way of seeing the world.*

5.3

To enable you to manage more diversity with less difficulty, understanding difference is not enough. You need to be able to translate this understanding into action. This activity gives you a first try at this.

Step 1   *Take one of the perspectives in the activity above that is not your own. Think about the way that person thinks and understands the world. Look for the value in that point of view.*

Step 2   *Imagine you are negotiating with such a person, or trying to influence them on a specific issue that you are familiar with: what kind of arguments would you need to bring forward?*

Step 3   *Plan how you might do that, and notice whether doing so enriches your own understanding in any way.*

Religious differences

Religious differences can be important in the way we engage with our lives and work. By this I do not mean the conflicts that arise between people of different religions, but the fundamental differences in beliefs about the world and about good and evil that may be present in different religions. Working in a group that contains a mixture of people who are committed to Christianity, Islam or Judaism may require a clear understanding of the external things such as religious holidays, but also the internal things that may affect priorities and decision-making. This may include the dynamic tension that arises between commitment to the organisation and commitment to the faith or cultural community to which individuals belong. The wise manager takes account of these, and finds ways to build synergy and balance between a clear focus on organisational goals and professional behaviour on the one hand, and the individual differences that both need to be allowed for, and which bring a richness to the group from which all can learn.

Some years ago I met a manager in a local authority housing office, who worked with a mixed team drawn from the community that the office served. As I waited to meet her, I was impressed by the highly professional atmosphere, and the efficient, friendly and respectful way they dealt with phone calls from people desperate for a house or flat. The team included housing officers from a wide variety of backgrounds, including Afro-Caribbean, whose families came originally from different islands, Sikh, Gujerati, and whites. There were clear differences in religion, age and educational background. In our discussion I asked her how she had built such a team, working as they were in stressful conditions in a small portakabin temporarily located in a school playground.

Her reply went like this. "Well first, it doesn't seem so strange to me. I grew up and went to school in an area like this, so I have always assumed people will be very different from each other, and it doesn't stop you from getting on with each other. Second, I'm very clear about our standards of service, and the professional ability of the people working here. And third, although I insist that all the housing officers must be able to handle any case, I'm also aware that some cases (such as Indian girls running away from arranged marriages, or single parents) will put more pressure on some staff than others because of their beliefs or their links in the community. And I take that into account in the way we allocate work."

I saw this as a good model for managing any diverse team, not only multicultural ones.

Understanding your own assumptions

If you have worked through the ideas in this chapter, you may have become clearer about your own assumptions and how rigidly or flexibly you hold to them. This is an essential first step in being able to work effectively with diversity. Sometimes the process of being in a business or personal relationship with a person with a very different view or way of behaving, who none the less is effective in what they do, brings home this understanding. It can certainly remind us that there are very many ways of achieving the same outcome. I often hear people say "I can't understand how they think they can do business like that!" about ways of working that are certainly different, and may even be based on different business values, but which succeed by any criteria. This cry is an indication of people who believe in their own way too rigidly to be free to observe the positive results of alternative ways.

Men and women working and talking together

The following is often particularly true of men and women working or living together. We could get tired of hearing "If only men would . . ." or "If only women would . . ." implying "If only the other person would be like me." Although we are in many ways more alike than we are different, some patterns of behaviour and ways of thinking are more commonly seen in women, and a different set are more commonly seen in men. We can save much energy, anger and frustration if we take account of some of these differences. Some years ago, at a conference on ways of bringing more women into management, Charles Handy remarked that male managers needed to be aware of two or three things about women in a generalised way. First, he said, they prefer to work with you rather than for you. Second, they quite rightly have a lot of other things going on in their lives that matter to them; this in no way detracts from the quality of their work and probably enhances it. He added a third factor: geography matters to them. They may want to be accessible to people who are dependent on them: their children, their parents or their grandchildren.

Deborah Tannen (1991), in her book *You Just Don't Understand*, (p. 17), says that there definitely are gender differences in ways of speaking, and that it is important to identify and understand them. "Without such understanding" she says, "we are doomed to blame others or ourselves – or the relationship – for the otherwise mystifying and damaging effects of our contrasting conversational styles." She suggests that many of the tensions or misunderstandings between men and women arise because the world of boys, in which men grow up, is different from the world of girls: they are essentially in different cultures, so talk between them can be seen as cross-cultural communication. Although communication problems do not account for all the misunderstandings between men and women, both at work and at home, they certainly contribute to many of the difficulties we have. Tannen suggests that both men and women engage in the contest for independence and success, as well as in the attempt to preserve intimacy and avoid isolation, but that the primary focus for men is that of achieving status and avoiding failure, and the primary focus for women is often that of achieving involvement and building connections. This becomes a problem when, as with the other differences we have discussed already, each assumes that their approach is the only one and the right one, and ascribe bad intentions to someone who is acting or thinking differently.

Tannen describes the difference between "public" and "private" speaking, and suggests that men feel more comfortable with "public speaking" or "report talk" as she names it which function is to preserve independence, exhibit knowledge and skill, and hold centre stage by imparting information or joking. Women, however, may be more comfortable with "private speaking", or "rapport talk" in her terms, which function is to establish connections and negotiate relationships, with the emphasis on displaying similarities and matching experiences. As well as this, men and women may have very different ideas of what is important enough to be discussed; talk for information or talk for interaction. The issues of communication are often the cause of misunderstanding and wasted energy at work and at home. Different conversational styles, or styles in meetings, can be very differently interpreted, as being enthusiastic/pushy and rude, polite/passive, verbose/picturesque, boastful/self-confident and so on, depending on the cultural background of the people talking and the people listening.

John Gray (1993) gives a good example of how in general ways men and women may react differently. In hearing about a difficult situation, the masculine response is to offer solutions, and the feminine response is to offer unsolicited advice and direction. In the face of stress, men, he suggests, tend to pull away and silently think about what is bothering them, while women feel an instinctive need to talk about it. This works when men are dealing with men, and women with women; but does not work so well across gender. Although he is writing about personal relationships, much of what he says is valid for working relationships.

In one view, there are masculine and feminine elements in us all, and to work and live effectively we need to find an appropriate balance. Some of the features described in the "left brain" list (Table 1.2 in Chapter 1) may be more predominant in men and need to be balanced by developing or valuing the "right brain" characteristics; and the "right brain" characteristics may be more accessible to women, who then may want to balance them by developing or valuing the "left brain" qualities in themselves.

What does all this mean for managing more with less? By observing, understanding and valuing the different approaches and ways of talking that men and women may bring, opportunities for working in a way that is in fact better for everybody will not be missed. Because until recently the workplace was mainly a male domain, where careers that attracted many women still had a predominance of men at the top, particular assumptions and ways of working have been dominant: beliefs and behaviour, for instance, about competition, about hierarchy and status. As the workplace is changing, and as the context of work is changing, including its globalisation, the balancing set of ways of working based on skills of cooperation, networks and involvement are increasingly required. When men and women can work together effectively, a balance is brought into the workplace that is able to be responsive to new situations, honours family commitments and draws the best from all participants; as does any well-managed multicultural setting.

Conclusion

It is time-consuming and wasteful to assume that everyone is or should be the same as us. It is also disabling to try and figure out in what ways everyone is different and to try to be what we think they want us to be. What is important is to understand more about ourselves and our own priorities and assumptions, and then to see to what extent they are challenged by other assumptions. Where there is no challenge, we can "agree to differ". Where there is a challenge, a difference that leads to misunderstandings or unproductive conflict, then it is necessary to develop an increased understanding, a sense of where there is a match in desired outcomes, even if not in ways of getting to those outcomes. Sometimes a compromise is necessary, but more often an overarching goal can be found in which the differences become not problems but ways of achieving a useful balance and arriving at a common goal.

Please note that this chapter only covers one approach to discrimination and opens more issues than can be covered here. For further information contact the following groups:

Employers' Forum for Disability;
Employers' Forum for Age;
Race for Opportunity;
Opportunity 2000;
Parents at Work.

All these groups are working across the areas of culture, policy and practice.

6 Understanding your relationship with time

Introduction

● Before starting this chapter, reflect on how you see time. If you had to represent the way you see past, present and future as three circles in some kind of relationship, what would you draw? What significance do the past, present and future have for you? How do you yourself represent time: is it in terms of your life, of time passing, of chunks of time, of hours minutes and days? What kind of clock, actual and metaphorical, are you living by? What does time mean to you?

● When we are working with multiple priorities, or complex situations, one of the pressures we feel comes from our attitude to time. Notice the language that is used about time. Sometimes it is spoken of as a commodity: "wasting time", "buying time", "insufficient time". Two questions come to mind "Can time be owned?" and "Does your employer own your time?" What is your opinion?

Using this chapter

For people working under pressure, there is not time enough to "do everything". In this situation, the traditional way of looking at time management, with lists, priorities and structures, may not be enough to deal with the overload or complexity. More understanding and different approaches are needed. This chapter will assume that you have at least tried, and preferably are using, some of the traditional techniques. For those that have not, a summary is included as the second part of the chapter. You may like to preview that section, using the points as a checklist. The first part of the chapter discusses different views of time and some of the assumptions we have about time, and how these affect our ability to manage under pressure.

"Plenty of time"

What does the phrase "all the time in the world" mean to you?

Once when I was shopping in a small village in the country, I could not find my cheque book, and held up the queue at the checkout while I searched through my purse for enough money. Embarrassed, I turned to the person behind me in the queue and said "I'm sorry to hold you up". "That's alright," she said to my astonishment, "I'm not in a hurry." For me, as a Londoner, down for a long weekend, her reply stopped me in my tracks. In her place, even though I was not in a hurry either, I would still have been restless and critical of this disorganised woman in front of me.

There are situations, we all know, where there is a real deadline: the last train out of an about-to-be occupied country; the journey to the hospital for someone having a heart attack; getting into the lifeboats before the ship sinks. In a less dramatic way, there are deadlines of meeting the contract deadline on a construction project, or the publication date in a journal. When under pressure in our everyday working lives, however, most of us use the adrenaline that would be necessary in life-and-death situations, feeling that urgent activity is the only way to deal with tight deadlines. This does not necessarily make us more effective, or enable us to meet the deadlines any better. A wider view of what we mean by time can help us to organise ourselves differently – meeting deadlines, but in a different way.

"One thing at a time" or "everything at once"

There are two particular concepts in ways of understanding time that may have an effect on the way you work and manage your life. In one way of thinking, we link past and future in the way they influence the present, and also feel comfortable with doing several things at the same time, in a kind of parallel processing or synchronous thinking. In the other way, we see time as a series of steps, of passing events, and are comfortable with doing things in order, "one thing at a time", sequentially. Individuals tend to have a preference for one approach or the other (it is said that in general men tend to favour the sequential and women the synchronous approach). In different situations one or the other will be more fitting.

6.1

Pause for a moment to reflect on your own approach to time, and where you learned it. The following questions can show the difference in assumptions that people can have about time. People with different assumptions will answer them differently, and with equal validity. For each question, when you have answered it, reflect on what your answer tells you about your assumptions about time.

Step 1

1. *What is your approach to*
   - *punctuality*
   - *deadlines*
   - *future planning*
   - *interruptions in what you do?*
2. *Do you see time as a resource to be managed, or an idea?*
3. *How do you see your past experience? In what way do you value it?*
4. *Do you plan for the future? If you do, do you expect these plans to come to fruition?*

UNDERSTANDING YOUR RELATIONSHIP WITH TIME

5. How do you schedule your time? Very efficiently, with no gaps between the slots and no wasted time, or with a certain amount of slack?

6. Do you think it is rude to be late? What in your opinion would justify being late? How do you feel about yourself if you are late and about other people if they are late?

7. Do you think it is rude or justifiable, to refuse to see someone because you are busy or it would interfere with your schedule?

8. At work, do you tend to deal with one thing at a time, or several?

Step 2   Discuss these questions and your answers with someone else, looking for your different attitudes and assumptions.

Result   Thinking things through like this can help you see that there are different ways of dealing with issues of time, some of which come from our cultural background.

There is an interesting chapter in Fons Trompenaars's (1993) book, *Riding the Waves of Culture*, which deals with this topic.

Time and timing

A story is told of two greenfield factory construction projects, both with an uncomfortably short time scale for completion. One was contracted to a British firm, and one to a Japanese firm. The clients in both cases were British.

On the first day, both contracting companies were visiting the site in the usual way. Soon after that, the bulldozers moved in to the British contractor's site and work started; the clients were very satisfied to see how quickly they started to get on with things. On the other site, nothing seemed to be happening. The Japanese contractors were nowhere to be seen. The clients visited the Head Office to see what was happening and were told that the team were out looking at local conditions and other factories, and talking to suppliers. "You realise there's a deadline and it must be met?" "Yes, it is a tight deadline," they were told, "It will be met". The client looked with envy at the other site where the access road was already being built.

Some weeks later, the British contractors were laying the foundations, and making some adjustments to the access road which needed to be widened. Still the Japanese firm appeared to be doing nothing. The British clients were getting increasingly anxious. They watched the British firm on the other site working hard, having some problems with the roof, certainly, but at least something was happening. Halfway through the allotted time, activity started slowly on the site with the Japanese contractors. Three-quarters of the way through the time, the British contractors site had a more or less complete factory, although they were having some problems with the flooring. The Japanese contractors began to work with great energy on the site; materials and machinery flowed in smoothly, and as if by magic the project was completed, ready to start manufacturing, two days before the deadline. The British contractors were also doing a good job, and they too had finished by the deadline; but had to come in a few times afterwards because of some problems with the lighting and ventilation and other small details.

And the moral is . . .?

One of the morals I draw from the story is that the less time we believe we have, the more important it is to use it well, and thinking things through effectively is one way of using it well. It is interesting too to see how differently the British team and the Japanese team valued "action" and getting on with things quickly compared to planning and thinking.

Preferences for action and time

I was working recently with a senior management team of a comparatively new and highly successful major charity. They were moving, or trying to move, from the start-up phase to a consolidated phase, and were having some problems with the transition. When they looked at their preferences for action in new or changing situations they were all but one in the category described by authors such as Honey and Mumford as pragmatist/activist, a preference for starting with concrete action. This was very effective in a high pressure start-up situation but not so helpful in a consolidation and development phase. Their preferred way of spending time was in "doing things". They had less appreciation of other important factors, and valued "doing something" above everything else.

6.2

You may like to try this activity.

Step 1   *Imagine you are in a new and challenging situation, in which you want to do well.*

Step 2   *If, as a **first** step, you had to choose between taking some concrete action or getting more information, a clearer picture of the situation, where would your preference lie, on the continuum below?*

Concrete action

Getting more information
frameworks, understanding the situation

Figure 6.1   Concrete action or more information?

Step 3   *If you then had a further choice, between making plans, trying things out, or reflecting on your experience, learning by observing, where would your preference lie on the following continuum?*

Planning   Reflecting

Trying new things   Observing

Figure 6.2   Planning and trying new things or reflecting and observing?

Step 4   *If you combine the two lines, you get a rough picture of where you prefer to start a new activity.*

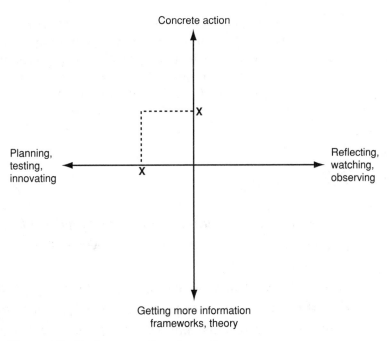

Concrete action

Planning, testing, innovating   Reflecting, watching, observing

Getting more information frameworks, theory

Figure 6.3   Placing yourself on the preference map

Step 5   *Reflect on the result and see if there are moments when this preference affects the way you manage your time.*

Step 6   *Consider your colleagues: where do you guess their preferences might be? How could you combine with them to be more effective? How could you widen your own preferences.*

UNDERSTANDING YOUR RELATIONSHIP WITH TIME

Result   *We all use all of these approaches in order to be effective. We differ however both in where we prefer to start, and in which aspects we value the most and want to spend time on. Doing this activity can help you see where your gaps are, and ways of developing your ability to select ways of spending time appropriately.*

Locating yourself in the flow of time

In the discussion so far, we are still treating time as a commodity, a fixed resource. Sometimes it is more useful to understand time in terms of rhythm, timing and timeliness.

Time can be considered as a flow of which you are a part. Thinking like this, you can engage with the passage of time in a more fluid way, looking at the long term and the short term, setting your priorities with a sense of your whole life as well as the day or hour that you are managing in at the moment.

6.3

This activity can be carried out at a fairly profound level which takes space and time. Here is an abbreviated form.

Step 1   *Looking back on your life, divide it in terms of eight to twelve different phases when certain things were happening to you or certain things seemed important, and name the milestones or turning points between those phases.*

Step 2   *Identify the flow of your interests and activity in those phases, covering aspects such as your work, your relationships, your creative activities, your interest in aspects of society.*

Step 3   *You may also find it interesting to look at the "roads taken and not taken"; choices you made at certain turning points. Often the "road* *not taken" still carries some interest or energy for you, and may come round again as an opportunity.*

Result   *This activity gives you the opportunity to take a longer view of time, and can give you a different view of the importance of current pressures that you experience as "not enough time". With this wider picture in view, you can reassess the way you are living your life, the flow of your experience, including your experience at work.*

Getting the facts about your activities

The above activity may encourage you to look at how you focused on different priorities at different phases in your life. Many authors recommend the use of a log in the daily activity of your life, to help you see what you actually do in terms of the time spent on it. Once you see the pattern, you are in a better position to make some choices about whether you want to continue in the same way. I have found that developing the habit of stopping and thinking "Is this what I want to be doing right now? What is it helping me to do? Why do I need to be doing this now?" helps me to make better choices, rather than getting caught up in activities that in retrospect were not what I wanted to be doing. A colleague of mine checked himself by using the phrase "Is this a high-yield activity?" applying the question both to his current work and to his life.

The project management techniques discussed in Chapter 2 are useful in deciding how to allocate your time and energy appropriately, maintaining an effective flow, particularly when you are working to a deadline. They can also help you to see to what extent the deadline you are working to is a realistic one, and challenge the time frame at the time the deadline is set rather than asking for an extension at the last minute. This is also true when you are allocating tasks to the people who work with you or for you. Discuss the time flow and be particularly clear about the milestones, review dates and delivery dates.

Consider too the rhythm and pace of the project; when will there be pressure, and when will there be breathing spaces.

UNDERSTANDING YOUR RELATIONSHIP WITH TIME

Your life as a project

There is a temptation to see one's life as a project with deadlines such as "By the time I am thirty . . ." This is helpful in one way, in terms of understanding the stages of your life, a sense of timeliness and transitions. It can be problematic when it leads to an unthinking driven behaviour, or comparing oneself with others, and omitting to clarify "Why?" Being perpetually self-driven to achieve greater heights is stressful. Unless you give yourself time to pause, review, rethink, it is hard to develop or maintain serenity or peace with yourself. It can also leave you with questions like "What was all that for?" and "Is that all there is?" Having achieved your goals, they do not feel particularly valuable.

The "project" approach to life can lead to a greater vulnerability to the inevitable losses and tragedies that are part of life, the discontinuities that hit "the plan". Human life involves losses and transitions, particularly in personal lives, and increasingly in organisational life. Loss and ending play a part in our understanding of living in time, and the pattern of our lives in time. Our "project", if we see our lives this way, needs to encompass this. When we begin to see recurrent challenges and crises as a valid part of everyday living rather than exceptions or failures, then we can make a different sense of our experience and life. This kind of shift can give us a glimpse of a different way where, in spite of distress and worry, life suddenly seems full of promise. This means abandoning the sense of needing or wishing to have control over our destiny. Paradoxically this reduces our fears of being at the mercy of fate. This glimpse can also help us to discover an inner connectedness to something greater than ourselves, a sense of the spiritual, and of wider possibilities in the way we live our lives.

Life as a school

Instead of the tendency to live life as a series of events, we can take an alternative view, which is to see life as a school, as a means of learning more about one's true self. Life is the teacher and you are the pupil. Seeing things this way shifts our experience of time.

If you find this an attractive or possible idea, try looking at a current dilemma, something you are trying to deal with, and ask yourself "If this was a lesson for me, what would it be about?" "How does this dilemma fit in with the patterns of my life?"

This can lead to a step forward in understanding what you are actually doing, which can greatly enhance your effectiveness. It helps you to let go of unnecessary internal conversations, of anxiety and of being too attached to the issue.

Time and change: transition periods

We become very aware of time, in a different way, when the rate of change increases or decreases. We are used to change, in terms of seasons, life stages, technological progress. What most of us find hard is a change in the rate of change, either changing faster or more slowly than we are used to. Our sense of rhythm is unsettled when change appears to accelerate continually without any pauses for consolidation or a new stability. In this situation it is essential to look for aspects of life current where the flow is different, more rhythmical, with more substance. This sometimes requires stepping back, and viewing the overall rhythm of the way organisations are developing, or your profession or occupation is changing; it may also require looking for a "timeless" aspect of life, to compensate for the "time-driven" flavour of working life. It may be useful to spend time in the country, more in touch with seasonal rhythms to provide a counter-balance and a reminder that there is another way of experiencing time. There is more about this in Chapter 7.

The transition process, moving from one state to another is often an uncomfortable process – seeing transition as a normal part of the flow of life, set in context, helps us manage the discomfort more productively. You can manage transitions with less discomfort if you understand the process. A colleague of mine, Maureen Cusick, described it to me in this way. "Think of three overlapping circles. The first one is the state you have been in, where you have some sense of who you are, some workable assumptions, some fairly clear definitions of how to succeed or be effective. Then, at the intersection of the first and second circle, something happens. The "something" is important because it has the effect of making the definitions less clear, and of challenging your assumptions. This shock can lead to a feeling of vulnerability and insecurity, even a sense of "who am I?" as well as a sense of anticipation and potential. I call it the "no person's land". In every case of transition, it is a zone of discomfort and also of growth.

When I looked back on the different phases of my life, I could recognise that "no person's land" – moving as a child from the country to London, where all the things I had taken for granted about roaming round free, being the eldest child in a little village school, were suddenly not viable. I loved London and still do but that first month or so after arriving in London was distinctly uncomfortable. I quickly learnt to define myself as a Londoner and that was fine until I went as a student to Edinburgh. I soon defined myself as a student and knew what to do, how to behave, how the world was – until I graduated and married and went to live in a recently post-colonial world in the tropics . . . and so it goes on.

Transitions are a normal and necessary part of growth, and so is the phase of discomfort. If the transitional phase happens to be extremely uncomfortable, the temptation is to reach back and hold on to old ways, or move too quickly into the next phase without exploring all the possibilities of the transition zone.

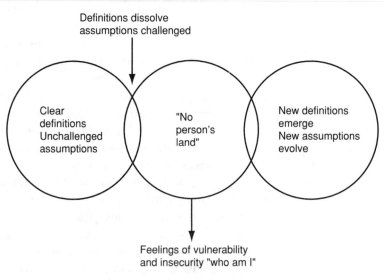

Figure 6.4 Stages in transitions. Maureen's picture

The trick seems to be, in managing transition, to know there may be a phase of discomfort and insecurity, and accept the experience for what it is. Manage the discomfort, rather than trying to avoid it, pathologise it or cure it.

This part of the chapter has focused on our understanding and experience of time. Within that we may need to manage our days more effectively, with less genuinely unproductive time.

Traditional time management tips and techniques

At the heart of good time management is the shift of focus of concentrating on results, not on being busy. These techniques are very useful, but more so when they are underpinned by the deeper understandings we have discussed above.

Tip 1: using a time journal (activity log)

- Keep a record, every 15 minutes, of what you do for a week at least.
- See what you find out about what you actually do during the working day, rather than what you think you do. Ask other people too.
- Then ask the questions:
    What am I doing that does not really need to be done?
    What am I doing that could be done by someone else?
    What am I doing that could be done more efficiently or effectively?
    What do I do that wastes others' time?

Tip 2: review your current patterns

- Use an activity log (see above) to evaluate your use of time, and your energy levels at different times of the day.
- Determine and agree what is important for success in your job, and what constitutes exceptional performance.
- Set goals and plans that will lead you to that success.

Tip 3: improve your resourcefulness

- Eat properly and rest effectively so that you spend more time performing well.
- Run and attend meetings effectively.
- If you have to wait, use the time to do other things such as planning, reviewing, writing.
- Improve your reading skills, learn to sift, skim, select: *and* throw away.
- Drucker's dictum: Doing things right is not as important as doing the right things.
- Check that you are looking for effectiveness – doing things that make a positive difference, rather than efficiency.
- Benefit/cost analysis: continue reviewing "Is this the most effective way of using my time and energy?"

Tip 4: delegate work to other people

Delegation involves passing responsibility for completion of work to other people.

Why you should delegate

- People can take responsibility for jobs you do not have time to do.
- People can look after routine tasks that are not cost-effective for you to carry out.
- It transfers works to people who can do things better than you.
- Your staff take more responsibility and can increase their enjoyment of their jobs.

Plan to reach the position where your staff carry out all the routine activities of your team, leaving you in a position to think and plan and improve the effectiveness of what you do. When delegating, make time to explain the job carefully.

What jobs to delegate

Choose jobs where:

- There is a certain margin of error allowable that can be corrected later.
- They could be more effectively or less expensively done by someone else.

- You have realised (perhaps through an activity log) that you are spending large amounts of time on low-yield jobs.
- Someone else (e.g. your secretary) knows more about it in reality than you do.

What to do to make sure delegation works

- Do it in steps, limited or small tasks first. Coach, encourage and give practice to others so that they improve their ability to carry out larger and larger tasks unsupervised.
- Delegate complete jobs. If you delegate a complete task to a capable assistant, he or she will get satisfaction and they are in a good position to achieve an elegant and integrated solution.
- When you delegate a job, be clear. Tell the person to whom you are delegating:
  - the results that are needed
  - the importance of the job and where it fits in to the overall work
  - who the other stakeholders are, if any
  - the constraints within which it should be carried out
  - the deadlines for completion
  - the help, if any, you can give and when
  - internal reporting dates, when you want information on progress.
- Remember that there may be different ways of achieving a particular task, and that yours is not necessarily the best.
- Be clear what the finished work will look like and do not accept partially complete work. If you accept only partially completed work back, then you will have to invest time in completing it and nothing will really have been achieved.
- Give support, help and coaching if people are having difficulties, but do not do the job for them. If you do, then they will not develop the confidence to do the job themselves.
- Remember that you need your people to learn, and they may need to learn through mistakes. Plan how you will manage this possibility.
- Give credit when a job has been successfully completed.
- See people as your assistants rather than your subordinates. Let them help you get the whole job done.

Be aware of what stops you from delegating, and deal with it

- Knowing that delegating jobs takes time, and attention. Jobs may take longer to achieve at first with delegation than they do for you to do by yourself, when coaching and checking are taken into account.
  (Cure: choose small tasks first that are easy to delegate.)
- Perfectionism – fear of mistakes.
  (Cure: work hard at setting clear and realistic criteria for how the finished job will look; at what exactly needs to have been achieved.)
- Enjoying "doing it myself".
  (Cure: bear in mind the cost of your time and the cost of your department's time when you are tempted to do a job yourself, and know when you are doing it to amuse yourself rather than for the sake of efficiency.)
- Fear of surrendering authority.
  (Cure: review your fears about loss of authority: to what extent are they based on your experience?)
- Fear of becoming invisible – "doing myself out of a job".
  (Cure: check it out; can you use the time and energy gained by delegating to start doing more visible activities?)
- Belief that staff "are not up to the job".
  (Cure: remember that good people will often underperform if they are bored or undervalued. Give it a try. Think about the effective lives they are probably leading outside work.)

It is common for people who are newly promoted to managerial positions to have difficulty delegating. Often they will have been promoted because they were good at what they were doing. This brings the temptation to continue trying to do their previous job, rather than developing their new subordinates to do the job well, and getting on with their own job thinking, planning and managing.

What should not be delegated (although it may be shared)?

- Your own responsibility for developing staff.
- Your strategic approach to the job.
- Thinking.

- Supporting staff.
- Jobs that genuinely cannot be done by someone else (although it is time you changed that!).

Tip 5: questions to ask and techniques to help you manage your time

- Why am I doing this?
- What is the goal?
- Why will I succeed?
- What happens if I choose not to do it?

- To do lists.
- Break things down into small steps.
- Do the ugliest thing first.
- Include a step towards a long-term goal.

Tip 6: look at your desk – what does it represent about you? (managing paperwork)

- Clutter leads to thrashing. Focus on one thing at a time for two hours a day.
- A good file system is essential.
- Touch each piece of paper once, then deal with it or bin it.
- Correspondence (letters and memos) – answer on the letter itself.
- Reading pile: "only read something if you'll be fired for not reading it".

Tip 7: managing the telephone

- Keep calls short; stand during call.
- Start by clarifying for yourself the purposes of the call.
- Tell the other person what the purpose of the call is. After the greeting, "I am calling to . . .".
- Know when to stop. When done, conclude firmly and get off.
- Group outgoing calls, just before lunch and 5 p.m.

Tip 8: saying yes to the person, saying no to the request

- Ask yourself, "If I say yes, in what way will this help me meet my goals?"
- Say yes to the person and no to the request. "I'm pleased you asked me. In principle I'd like to help. It's not possible at the moment."

Tip 9: remember everyone has good and bad times

- Find your creative/thinking time. Defend it ruthlessly, spend it alone if that is what works for you, maybe at home. If you need other people around to be creative and think well, be sure that you do not waste the time in socialising.
- Find your dead time. Schedule meetings, phone calls and mundane stuff during it. And then "just do it".

Tip 10: minimise interruptions

- "I'm in the middle of something now . . ."
- Start with "I only have 5 minutes . . ." you can always extend this.
- Stand up, move to door, compliment, thank, shake hands.
- Act in such a way that the interruption is useful to both of you.

Tip 11: deal with procrastination

How and why do you procrastinate?

- By overemphasis on planning, where the planning process is drawn out to avoid confronting an issue.
- By inappropriate perfectionism, spending time in polishing plans instead of starting to carry them out.
- By spending too long on making the results perfect rather than moving on to the next phase. Often perfection simply is not required, and is not cost-effective to achieve.
- By thinking that certain jobs will be boring or difficult, and putting them off for spurious reasons rather than facing up to them.
- By giving in to hostility; where you are hostile to the person who is giving you the task; and letting your pride prevent you from getting on with it.
- By getting addicted to the "deadline adrenaline", and liking the drama of finishing at the last moment, even though it could have been finished with time to spare without the earlier procrastination.

6.4 Review your time management skills

Review and assess your time management skills. What thinking, strategies and behaviours do you currently use to:

- ○ *be selective about what you do*
- ○ *be prepared for meetings*
- ○ *refuse excessive workloads*
- ○ *be clear about what you are trying to achieve*
- ○ *monitor project progress*
- ○ *allocate resource (time) appropriate to a task's importance*
- ○ *ensure that long-term projects are not neglected*
- ○ *plan each day efficiently*
- ○ *plan each week effectively*
- ○ *maintain your self-discipline?*

Conclusion

As well as managing time in the here and now, to be effective we need a deeper sense of what we mean by "time" and how it relates to the overall pattern and experience of our lives.

In this chapter, we have looked at the way you understand time and the effect that this may have on you. We have also looked at time in terms of timing, pacing and flow, and individual preferences for action in time. Understanding time may include looking at the phases of your life, and what your priorities have been in those phases and in the transitions. At the end of the chapter is a summary of time management tips and techniques.

To manage our lives effectively, we must keep our main aim in mind, and maintain a balance between how we live and produce each day and our ability to live in the way that we want in the future.

Between stimulus and response in human beings lies the power to choose. This choice is one of the secrets of time management. Widen the moment and make the choices that work for you, and match what you really want with the time you experience. This means, as has been said in other chapters, being clear about what matters most to you in your life and using this frame of reference to make your day-to-day decisions.

Good personal decisions involve more than logic. We may want something that seems illogical, yet it still feels right for us to choose it. It is the successful integration of logic and emotion that makes personal decision-making properly grounded and effective.

It is well known that people who enjoy a sense of control in their lives also enjoy better health – because they have freed themselves from the stress of outside pressures. Developing a philosophical as well as a practical sense of your relationship to time will help you both manage time effectively as a "resource" and also engage with the flow of time as you experience it in your life as a whole, balancing the notion of control of your time with that of the pattern and flow of time in general.

7 Looking after yourself – your greatest asset

Introduction

● Most of us are aware what it is like when we are not looking after ourselves properly, when we are going on with diminishing returns, losing a sense of who we are, working with increasingly tunnel vision and a feeling of helplessness. We can also be aware of what we are like when we are looking after ourselves, when we have a sense of being nourished by an inner kindness to ourselves and other people, with permission to grow, move forward and be our real selves. This chapter is meant to give you a better ability to be aware when you are not looking after yourself and when you are, and to help you make it more possible to look after yourself in a way that helps you live your life to the full, contributing to your own development and to the life of people around you. Even when in difficult situations we need to be aware that we have some choices, at least about how we experience what is happening.

How to use this chapter

In this chapter we look at different aspects within the general topic of looking after yourself, such as dilemmas and choices, and how we deal with them; how to widen your view by watching other people; how to look after yourself physically with diet, exercise, sleeping, breathing; how to reconnect with your own values, knowing what they are and feeling comfortable working with them; and then feeling it possible to make the changes that you can make. Read through the whole chapter, allowing yourself time to engage with the different suggestions, finding which ones give you a feeling of possible enrichment. Then take some time to consider one or two of the ideas in some depth.

Dealing with dilemmas and choices

If you only have 2 options you have a dilemma. To have choices you must have at least 3 options.

You can learn a lot about how you look after yourself by reviewing how you behave, how you feel, what you do when you feel you are caught in an impossible situation, or when you feel you do not have a choice; when you feel you are trapped "on the horns of a dilemma".

Ironically, it is often the case that the time when we most need to be at our best, in order to deal with difficult situations or make difficult choices, is in fact the time when we do not look after ourselves, so that we are not in form to make those kind of challenging decisions. In this chapter we will be suggesting that you pay more attention to bringing yourself up to speed strengthening yourself as a resource so that when you have to do difficult things you are doing it from a position of health rather than from a position of fragmentation.

7.1

Step 1 *Think of a moment when you felt that you had less choice than you would like, or that you were caught in a dilemma of two equally unattractive choices.*

Step 2 *Looking back, notice how you dealt with that situation.*

○ *What did you do?*
○ *What was your inclination to action? How did you treat yourself?*

○ *If you worried, recall how you dealt with that worry and what that worry meant to you.*

○ *How did you react to perceived pressures from others?*

Result *This activity helps you to get a fuller awareness of what happens to you when you feel you are stuck with a dilemma or impossible choices, and what happens to your sense of yourself and your ways of caring for yourself while dealing with dilemmas. This deeper understanding may trigger some ideas about what you need to pay particular attention to.*

7.2

Step 1 *Think of a current dilemma or difficult choice you have to make.*

Step 2 *Notice if you are phrasing your dilemma in terms of "either/or".*

Step 3 *Think what would be a first small step, in getting more information about the implications of either choice.*

Step 4 *If you are thinking in terms of either/or, find a possible third alternative, which is neither one nor the other, possibly both or possibly something completely different.*

Step 5 *Enlarge this by (without evaluating them) writing down all the possible things a person might do in this situation. Notice the temptation, when you think of an option, to immediately think why you could not do it rather than allow it a little bit of peace and time to be explored.*

Step 6 *Stop, reflect, review your options, and notice how the process has affected you.*

LOOKING AFTER YOURSELF – YOUR GREATEST ASSET

Result   *Times of pressure or of having to make difficult choices are often the very times when we do not use the thinking or option-generating processes that would help us make those choices in a robust and human way. This activity helps you avoid this trap.*

Self-esteem and effectiveness

Self-esteem is an emerging topic in the self-help world, with an implicit assumption that it is important to build up your self-esteem in order to cope with life's difficulties. In my experience that is not always possible; it is probably, to begin with at any rate, more useful to decide to do what you need to do, with or without self-esteem. Believing that you have to feel good about yourself in order to be effective may handicap you.

Is there a substitute for self-esteem? In my view there is. It is a matter of just doing what needs to be done at the time regardless of how you particularly feel about it, a loosening of the line between how you feel and what you do. David Reynolds (1984) gives a nice set of examples of a young person blighted in love who sits in his or her room feeling that their world is at an end; the room is in a terrible mess and they feel even worse because the room is such a mess. He describes this as Stage One.

He says the second stage is when a person who is feeling terrible might notice that the room is in a mess, and tidy it because at least it might make them feel better, which it does a little.

The third level is when a person sitting in their room feeling terrible notices that the room is in a mess, and tidies the room because it needs tidying, not in order to make themselves feel better.

In my experience taking the approach of "doing what needs to be done now" helps people to be effective even if they have low self-esteem, or if their self-esteem has just taken a knock. As well as improving your self-esteem so as to put yourself in a position to make good choices or deal with difficult dilemmas from a position of courage, resource and feeling good about yourself, it is also possible to do something about it by doing what needs to be done now.

Reconnecting with your values

An important aspect of looking after yourself both in difficult times but also in easy times is from time to time to consider the questions: "Is this what I want to be doing? Is this what matters in my life?" To do this, of course, it is important to have some sense of what does matter in life, what your true values are. By this I mean, not the values that you would like to have, or think you have, but the values that you appear to live by. If there is a gap between what you seem to be living by and what you would like to be living by, it is important to stop and think and reconnect with what does matter to you. We all need to find ways of living our values in the world, even if only in a small way.

activity

7.3 Values clarification

Step 1   *Table 7.1 shows a list of 50 possible values, 50 things that might matter to a person. Choose five to ten values that are the most important to you in your life, and perhaps add one or two that are not on the list.*

Table 7.1   List of possible values

- ❏ Peace in the world, harmony between nations
- ❏ Going for excellence in all I do
- ❏ Secure income
- ❏ Relationship with God
- ❏ Exploring and discovering new things
- ❏ Loving family relationships
- ❏ Security and safety
- ❏ Creating art or music – using my creative gifts
- ❏ Developing my fullest potential
- ❏ Peace with the people around me – family and neighbours
- ❏ Providing adequately for my family
- ❏ Full enjoyment of life
- ❏ Seeking a satisfying sexual relationship
- ❏ Preserving biological diversity
- ❏ Having some power to do good
- ❏ Competition with others, striving to be the best

Table 7.1 (*Continued*)

- ☐ Seeking inner security
- ☐ Finding satisfaction in whatever life brings
- ☐ Valuing the differences between people and between nations
- ☐ Being surrounded by beautiful objects
- ☐ Happiness, health and safety of my children
- ☐ Following God's call
- ☐ Advancement of knowledge
- ☐ Achieving self-sufficiency
- ☐ Helping other people
- ☐ Knowing that I am living in the way that God wants me to in every area of life
- ☐ Tithing
- ☐ Sharing good fortune with others
- ☐ Thirst for scientific knowledge
- ☐ Having a successful business
- ☐ Maintaining an honourable reputation
- ☐ Leaving something substantial behind me when I die
- ☐ Being well known in the world
- ☐ Connecting with nature and preserving it
- ☐ Cleanliness and orderliness
- ☐ Keeping promises
- ☐ Doing my duty in all circumstances
- ☐ Keeping my body at its peak of fitness
- ☐ Appreciating the good things in life such as food and wine
- ☐ Being rich and staying rich
- ☐ Showing pride in my country
- ☐ Working honourably and ethically
- ☐ Belief in the value of working hard
- ☐ Achieving a good education for myself or my children
- ☐ Leaving a will
- ☐ Leaving my affairs in order

Others _____

_____

_____

_____

_____

_____

_____

Step 2 *Of the ones that you have chosen write them in the order in which you live them in your life; that is, the one you most obviously live by, as demonstrated by your actions at the top of the list.*

The things that you appear to do or live by most should come first and the things that you may value but do not actually live by or put into your actions should come at the bottom of your list.

Step 3 *Looking at the values that you adhere to, reflect on where you learned them, how it came about that these were your values. Bear in mind that you may have got them from your school, from your family, from your religion or spiritual life, from close friends or from the social group that you live in and work in. Read through the list of values you have identified as yours and see if any of them were generated by you yourself, as a result of your experience of life or in moments of reflection.*

Step 4 *Look at how you behaved in the last six weeks and the choices you made in terms of how you chose to spend your time, how you chose to deal with other people, how you prioritised your actions and your way of working. Generate a list of about five values which a person seeing the choices you made might assume were the ones you lived by.*

Step 5 *Give yourself a moment to look at how your values have evolved from when you first started work until now, and get a sense of how they may be evolving at this very moment and moving forward into the future. Bring to mind things that have become important to you recently, that you would make choices in favour of, that you would prioritise over other things that used not to be so important to you. Make a note of what these emerging values seem to be. Remember a value is something which informs the way you choose to behave.*

Engaging in your own life stages

As you may have seen in the previous section our values change and develop as we have a wider experience of life or have different things happening to us. This idea of how your values evolve and how you look after yourself can be enriched by paying more attention to the stage of your life that you are at. In terms of how much responsibility you are taking, how old you are, what transitions you are going through both in your personal and professional life, Table 7.2 may be of interest. If it does not match your experience of life, as it may not, see if you can draw a similar table for yourself of the life stages you have gone through so far and the ones that you anticipate coming next. The purpose of doing this is to give yourself a sense of being in a flow of a real life, and a life that belongs to you and over which you have a certain amount of control and power, even if it is only control and power about how you experience that life.

If you develop an understanding of the pattern of your own life as, in a way, your own art form (something that you are creating for yourself within the limits of the context around you, and your own personality), you may find that you get a sense of richness or of wholeness that is of great help in looking after yourself. For some people this goes along with developing a sense of inner stillness, of a calm peace within themselves.

Developing an inner stillness

There are other ways of achieving an inner stillness. One approach is to pay attention to very small details of everyday physical activities, whether it is cutting up vegetables, folding paper or even the experience of walking. This helps you to focus on the details of those kinds of activities. Do them as carefully and effectively and quietly as you can, as a way of stilling your mind.

Meditation is another route. Good explanations of this are given in *The Calm Technique* (1995) of different ways that suit different personalities, of arriving at that inner still peace.

Table 7.2 Stages and tasks of adulthood: where are you? Does this pattern describe your life?

Stages	Ages	Task
	16	
Pulling up roots		Separation from family
		Autonomy
		Self-sufficiency
	20	
		Getting into adult world
		Select career, make relationships
Provisional adulthood		Become member of organisation – inclusion
		Achieve place in society
		Exploration – trying many things
	28	
		First major reappraisal
		Re-examination of initial commitments re career and marriage
Age 30 transition		Reassess future objectives
		Life looks more complex
	32	
		Growing out of illusions
		Widening, depending and stabilising commitments
Rooting		Establish long-term goals, get career recognition
		Issues to do with parenting
		Get our heads down
	39	
		Come to terms with ageing – face mortality
		Re-examinaton of career and personal relationships
Mid-life transition		Deciding importance of work in life
		Assess gap between achievement and aspirations
		Relive adolescent conflicts
		Sense of limits: before everything was possible
	45	
		Autonomy
		Deepening of skills in technical role
		Taking on more responsibility
Restabilisation and flowering		Becoming a mentor
		Reopening after period of closure
		Acceptance of time as finite
		Can feel like best time of life
	55	
		Relative stability
Mellowing and renewal		Acceptance of what one has
		Fewer personal relationships
		Enjoyment of here-and-now
	65+	
		Dealing with retirement
		Adjusting to death of spouse/friends
		Preparing for own death

In the overall life cycle we can detect a repeating pattern of:

Career growth – excitement and challenge
Stabilisation – high performance
Transition – reassessment and anxiety

Widening your view

An important aspect of looking after yourself is, whilst keeping sight of yourself and what you are doing and how you are living, to set yourself in the wider context of what is happening in your society or in the world. This can be seen partly as a "count your blessings" activity but, more importantly, it reconnects you with real life and how the world is, rather than how you would like it to be. There are two aspects of this. One is to give yourself an opportunity to see some of the delights of the world, whether it is in looking at nature, surfing, whale watching or going for bicycle rides in the country. The other aspect is to understand how difficult life is for many people, including perhaps yourself. Meet people who are dealing with difficult lives and are coping with them with courage and resilience as a kind of example to yourself or a reminder of what real living can be like. We see people who are managing very difficult lives with very slender resources, both psychologically and materially, and we can learn a great deal from them, whether it is people living in shanty towns in Nicaragua or people that we know living on slender pensions, looking after disabled children or in other ways managing a rich and important commitment to life without having resources behind them.

A way of furthering this is by looking at your own life and looking at the difficult times that you have been through and how you have coped with them. Give yourself a moment to think of things that you have coped with that were difficult at least to you, and that you faced up to and came through, experiences that you can value because they made you the person that you are today. In the same vein, look at the things that you do contribute already to the richness of life to yourself and to other people, and how you might increase that contribution without using a lot more energy and time but just by enriching the small things that you do do with more awareness, more mindfulness, more consideration for what is going on in other people's lives.

NEW SKILLS PORTFOLIO

One thing stirs me when I look back at my youthful days; it is the fact that so many people gave me something or were something to me without knowing it. Such people had a decisive influence on me; they entered into my life and became powers within me. Much that I should not

otherwise have felt so clearly, or done so effectively, was felt or done as it was because I stand, as it were, under the sway of these people. Hence I always think that we all live spiritually by what others have given us in the significant hours of our life. These significant hours do not announce themselves as coming, but arrive unexpectedly. Nor do they make a great show of themselves; they pass almost unperceived. Often, indeed, their significance comes to us first as we look back. Much that has become our own in gentleness, modesty, kindness, willingness to forgive, in veracity, loyalty, resignation under suffering, we owe to people in whom we have seen or experienced these virtues at work, sometimes in a great matter sometimes in a small. A thought which had become act sprang into us like a spark and lighted a new flame within us. If we had before us those who have thus been a blessing to us, and could tell them how it came about, they would be amazed to learn what passed over from their life to ours.
(*Memories of Childhood and Youth*, Albert Schweitzer)

Looking after yourself physically

This is something which we can easily forget to do, even in a setting where we have enough food and we have enough money, with opportunities of being extremely healthy compared to people living, for instance, in poverty or very adverse conditions. It is important perhaps not to make a fetish of fitness or diet but to be mindful about the benefits that good eating, adequate exercise, good restful sleep and appropriate breathing can carry for you.

Exercise

Exercise has the effect both of improving the blood flow to your brain and the rest of your body, thus carrying the oxygen needed to help you function and carrying away the toxins that collect. Exercise also stimulates the production of endorphins, hormone-like substances which lead to a feeling of well-being. As well as this, it looks as though regular modest exercise increases your long-term health. A study of 3,000 women and 10,000 men conducted at the Institute for Aerobics Research in Dallas, USA, suggested that for people who took on even a slight increase in exercise, for instance a brisk walk for half an hour every day, there was a significantly reduced risk of dying from heart disease and cancer.

7.4

Step 1   *Review the exercise that you currently take.*

- ○ *Is it fun?*
- ○ *Does it fit easily into your schedule?*
- ○ *Are other "fitness" activities part of your daily life (e.g. walking up stairs)?*

Step 2   *If you are disinclined to take exercise reflect on why this is?*

- ○ *Do you tell yourself you are too busy?*
- ○ *Do you dislike exercise?*
- ○ *Do you suffer from a condition, such as asthma, which makes some exercise difficult?*

Make yourself some suggestions about small amounts of exercise that you could take, such as yoga, early morning stretching, walking one bus stop further on, tensing and flexing muscles while sitting down. Consider one small step you could take to reduce whatever it is that makes you disinclined to take enough exercise to keep you fit.

Step 3   *If exercise has become almost an obsession:*

- ○ *Notice when it started.*
- ○ *Notice what causes you to take so much exercise and what you fear might happen if you stopped.*
- ○ *Review the price you may be paying, i.e. opportunities missed by focusing so strongly on exercise as part of your life.*

Result   *Thinking things through in this way makes it possible for you to choose to take the amount of exercise that is appropriate for your metabolism and life style.*

Sleep

Sleep that knits up the ravelled sleeve of care . . .

There is sweet music here that softlier falls
Than petals from blown roses on the grass;
Than night dews on still waters between walls
Of shadowy granite in a gleaming pass;
Music that softlier on the spirit lies
Than tired eyelids upon tired eyes,
Music that brings sweet sleep down from the blissful skies.
(*Song of the Lotus Eaters*, Tennyson)

Many of us, in the face of complex work or conflicting priorities tend to try and manage with less sleep. It is not the length of sleep but its quality that makes it possible for us to manage more challenges and manage them well. Whatever the quality, however, we need a certain minimum, as anyone who has tried to work after the four hours sleep their fretful baby allowed them will know. Catching up on sleep helps – sleep on the train or plane; take a cat-nap or an afternoon sleep at the weekend.

If insomnia is the problem, try some or all of these:

- No alcohol before bedtime – it is a stimulant.
- Mild exercise early in the evening.
- No caffeine drinks after 6 p.m.
- Go to bed at a regular time.
- Reflect on something peaceful and satisfying as you go to bed.
- Slow down your breathing, imagining the air going slowly in and out, as you get ready for bed.
- Do not panic – it is possible to give yourself insomnia by worrying about insomnia!
- Try seeing a homeopath, who may be able to give you a balancing remedy.
- Eat a light snack, bread or fruit, an hour or two before you go to bed – avoid late sugary snacks or heavy meals.

Dreams as a resource

There are many views about the meaning or relevance of dreams. There is is no doubt, however, that they can provide a different lens for you, and can help you to pay attention to aspects you are ignoring in your waking life.

LOOKING AFTER YOURSELF – YOUR GREATEST ASSET

activity

7.5

This is a way of integrating a dream into the reality of your waking life. You need a dream that has stayed in your mind.

Step 1   *Recall the dream and its different aspects.*

Step 2   *Recall and write down what you felt.*

Step 3   *Taking each person or item in the dream, describe what happened as if you yourself were that component. "I am the house in the dream and . . .", "I am the moon in the dream and I see . . .", write it down.*

Step 4   *Make a note of anything that occurs to you, relevant or irrelevant, as you carry out Step 3.*

Step 5   *Now break away from the dream. Think of something that is occupying you or preoccupying you. Allow your mind to combine it with the dream in an imaginative way.*

Result   *You may get a new or deeper insight into the issue you are dealing with.*

Diet

Hungry or malnourished people do not bring their best resources to managing difficult situations. To make your life easier and you more effective, good and appropriate nutrition is essential. This means maintaining a balance in the food you eat of what is nutritious and what pleases and comforts you. It means eating fresh foods that still contain their vitamins, and eating raw foods that make you chew. It means drinking plenty of good quality water, and not very much coffee or tea.

Mind-sets and approaches to taking care of yourself

Even in the area of our physical well-being, we may be affecting the outcomes by the way we think about it.

What kind of a person are you in terms of how you deal with looking after yourself? Do you work from rules and self-discipline? Are you nourishing and looking after yourself in a nurturing way? Are you engaged in good eating and good exercise from a sociable point of view to link with other people? Do you do it just for fun of it? Are you strongly influenced by what other people are doing? Do you do it as an example for other people?

Which of the ways of thinking in Figure 7.1 do you think matches you most?

Figure 7.1 Thinking about fitness

LOOKING AFTER YOURSELF – YOUR GREATEST ASSET

Checklist

Listed below are some of the things which are considered to contribute to reduction in stress and increased resistance to infection, to enhance your immune system and bring you better sleep. Which do you know about and which do you use?

Diet

Antioxidants, vitamins and minerals.
Food combining diet (Hay diet).
Macrobiotic diet.
Eliminating certain foods because of allergies.
Exercise at least half an hour two times a week.
Making your heart beat.
Increasing stamina.
Increasing flexibility.

Sleep

What to do before sleep.
Importance of dreaming.
Using aromatherapy.
Using exercise to help you sleep.
Dealing with worry.
Getting up early.
Arranging the bedroom.

This may suggest things you want to find out more about.

Arranging your environment to make it supportive

The principles of feng shui, the Chinese art of managing space and your environment, can give us clues about ways of harmonising our environment and bringing it into balance. It is described as a way of seeing the world. It matches our growing understanding of the effect of micro and macro environments of individual health and well-being, and the need to integrate our outside world with our own "inner space". Like acupuncture, it is based on ideas of energy flows and ways of removing blockages to the flow. Used wisely, these principles can help us to create environments that are suitable for their intended activity by providing a balance at a variety of levels. It takes a common-sense approach to arranging or responding to the space around you, and to clearing up clutter.

As well as this, the ideas relate to a more mystical level, which some people are understandably sceptical about although those that try them in a spirit of experiment often report very good results. The methods, which sometimes seem esoteric, provide a final design that respects the people in it, and incorporates the principles of the whole world, not just the technological aspects. This involves paying attention to light, sound, living objects, intuition and subtle energy flows.

7.6

This is a taster activity. Feng shui is not a superficial philosophy, and if you find the idea interesting it is important to talk to someone with expertise.

This activity invites you to consider eight areas of your life, and see which ones need attention or are causing you unease or discomfort. You can then relate them to areas of your house or office and reflect on whether you can find any resonances.

Step 1   *Consider the following. To what extent are they satisfying and enriching or on the other hand problematic or absent.*

1. *The work you are doing and the current flow of your career.*
2. *Your close, significant relationships at the moment and your social life.*
3. *Your relationship with your parents, either in real life if they are alive, or in your memory if they are dead.*
4. *Your material situation: money and good fortune.*
5. *Your network of friends or helpers, close or distant, that you can depend on and who can depend on you.*
6. *Your sense of creativity; children, projects, ideas.*

7. *Your spiritual understanding, sense of the sacred or of mystery, ability to find an inner stillness.*

8. *Your reputation and the effect you have on others, what illuminates you.*

Step 2   *Consider how you would like each of these areas of your life to be, ideally. Visualise each as clearly as you can. Find your own way of describing what you want for yourself in each area. Give yourself the opportunity of imagining that that is how it is, experiencing in your own mind how you would really like it to be.*

Step 3   *Decide which areas of your life need most improvement or most attention.*

7.7

This is a follow-on activity from the previous one.

Step 1   *The "bagua". Consider the "map" in Diagram 7.2, as if it was a map of how your life is at the moment, using your responses from the previous activity. Remind yourself of the areas that you decided needed most attention.*

Step 2   *Imagine you were overlaying this map on to the plan of your office or workspace, lining up the wall which has the door in with the side of the bagua with 8, 1 and 6 in it. An example of a "bagua" overlaid over a house is shown in Diagram 7.3.*

Step 3   *Notice what kind of objects are in each of the areas, and what that might represent. If that area of your life was really being represented by the objects and the way they are arranged, what changes for the better might you make? Where is your untidiest part? Where do you have the best light or most attractive items?*

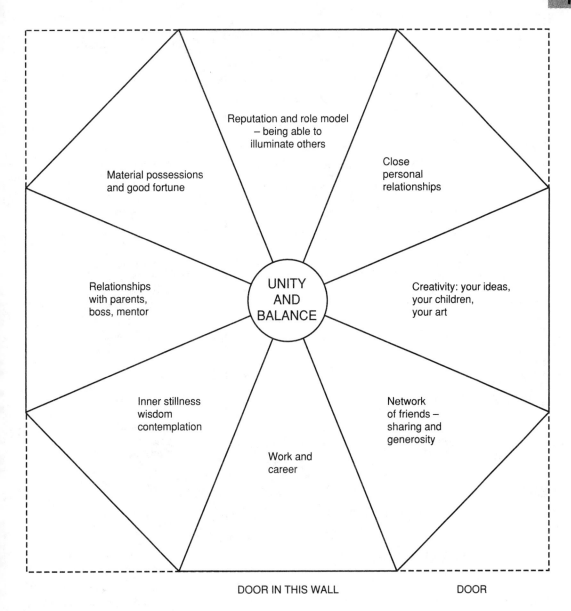

Reputation and role model
– being able to
illuminate others

Close
personal
relationships

Material possessions
and good fortune

UNITY
AND
BALANCE

Creativity: your ideas,
your children,
your art

Relationships
with parents,
boss, mentor

Inner stillness
wisdom
contemplation

Network
of friends –
sharing and
generosity

Work and
career

DOOR IN THIS WALL   DOOR

Figure 7.2   The map (the "bagua")

Result   *Carrying out this activity gives you a chance to assess the whole of*
your life, and what is needed to get back or maintain its balance.
Using the office as a metaphor by overlaying the "bagua" on it,
gives you the opportunity to make symbolic improvements that will
not only improve the office, but may resonate with improvements in
the balance of your life.

LOOKING AFTER YOURSELF – YOUR GREATEST ASSET

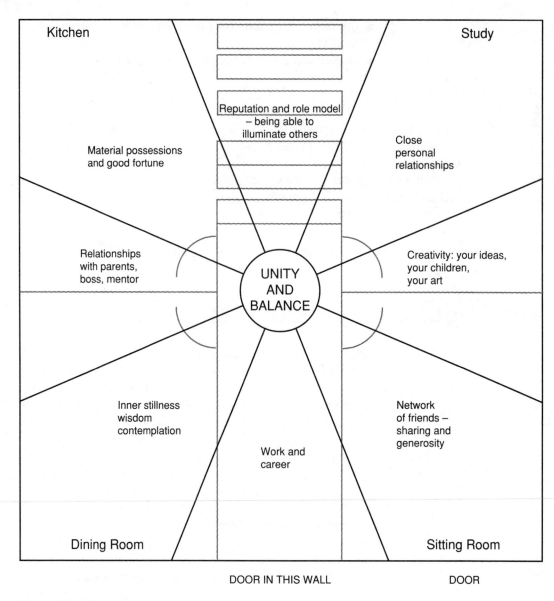

Figure 7.3 The "bagua" fitted over a house

Quite apart from the philosophy underlying feng shui, there are several common-sense approaches to improving the quality of your working environment that will save time energy and stress. These include:

- the position of the desk (parallel to the wall, backed by a solid wall)
- the lighting (bright enough but not glaring)

- ornaments or plants (not overpowering and attractive to look at)
- clutter and rubbish (get rid of it every day).

Inner Space

Thirty spokes in the wheel's hub
It is the centrehole that makes it useful.
Shape clay into a vessel
It is the space within that makes it useful.
Therefore profit comes from what is there
Usefulness from what is not there

What meaning does this poem carry for you?

The importance of laughter

Laughter has physiological, emotional and intellectual bene-fits. Having a good laugh relaxes the muscles and improves the breathing. When we are really laughing, other things fade away from the mind, and the joke and the laughter fill our consciousness even if only for a moment. This leaves us relaxed. As well as this, as Daniel Goleman (1996) suggests in *Emotional Intelligence* (p. 85), laughing "seems to help people think more broadly . . . recognising complex relation-ships and foreseeing the consequences of a given decision". He goes on to say how important mood is in the way we think, with a good mood leading to more expansive thinking. This suggests that the habit of looking for the humour in a situation is an unconscious way of looking after oneself, and can be carried through to deliberately seeing a funny film or video when things are tough or decisions are to be made.

Balancing being and doing

One of my colleagues uses the phrase "Remember you are a human being not a human doing". He uses it to remind people of the importance of balancing activity with more reflective ways of being, and the importance of coming back to yourself and finding a stillness, even if only for a moment. He is an example of this in his own life, having achieved a great deal, not without stress, but always able to share a sense of quietness and calm even when he is under pressure.

Alan Watts (1992), in *The Wisdom of Insecurity*, reminded us that there are two ways of experiencing the present moment; one is to compare it with previous moments and identify what we are experiencing, for example "I feel lonely" or "I feel under pressure". The other way is to be fully in the experience as a new experience, with all its uncertainties and unpredictabilities. He suggested that we try the experiment of being completely "in the moment", experiencing what is happening to us while not resisting it or defining it.

7.8

This is a brief activity that can be used to decrease stress and increase awareness.

Step 1   *Pause for a moment in whatever you are doing and focus your concentration momentarily inwards.*

Step 2   *Consider the following: who and what are you in this present moment, as you read this book? Attend to your breathing, your body, your thoughts, the texture of your clothes, the sounds around you. Let yourself become absorbed in the moment.*

The concept of "non-attachment"

This concept is described in various ways by the great religions, most familiarly in Buddhism. It is also relevant for those without commitment to a particular spiritual path. In brief, the idea reminds us that we may have an exaggerated desire for or hatred of certain things, which distorts our experience and ties us too closely to those things. Non-attachment is not the same as detachment. Non-attachment, as I understand it, involves a full commitment to the world and normal life, without an overly emotional involvement in things. We can care deeply about our children if we have them, without wanting to control them or hold on to them. This is a step towards non-attachment.

We can be interested in earning money, without being afraid of losing it, or avid to gain it, or actively despising it. This also is a step towards non-attachment. It seems to involve an acceptance of oneself, a freedom from the "ought to"s of industrial life in a way that is energising and delightful. This approach does not discount human suffering but sees it in a different light, within a bigger picture.

Conclusion

This chapter has covered a wide and eclectic range of ways of looking after yourself. It has brought the emphasis to you as an individual with an inner life and physiological needs. This has to be seen as one element of the two-sided nature of human beings: as individuals with a responsibility to themselves, and as members of a group or system to which they contribute, and which supports them. Chapter 9 suggests ways of managing the other side of the balance.

8 Developing your potential

Introduction

● When you are working under pressure, with what appears to be few choices, it is easy to get into a situation of diminishing returns – more and more effort with less satisfaction or learning.

● This chapter is about managing your own learning and development in the easiest way for yourself. This involves the initially challenging step of taking responsibility for your own learning, putting yourself as it were in the driving seat. It also involves being aware of what you have already learnt, and are learning now. As well as this, the chapter will provide you with ways of becoming clear about what learning or development you are looking for, for work and career, and perhaps also in your life outside work.

● Until recently, many people relied on "outside" organisations to train, educate or develop them. For example their company provided training programmes or they studied at college. These opportunities are less available and it is necessary to take a more active role themselves.

Using this chapter

To get the most out of this chapter, read it as a learner. Focus your attention on the reality of all your successful experiences of learning, reconnecting with your own astuteness and ability to learn, from childhood until now. This does not necessarily mean "school" learning. I remember asking my son, aged 9, what he had learned at school that day. "Nothing" he said, as usual. "Come on, you must have learned something!" "Well, yes," he replied, "I learned not to trust Frank Smith when he's playing hide and go seek". Social learning like this is as important as professional or academic learning.

There is a strand of our life experience which is dedicated, consciously or unconsciously to learning. To get the most from this chapter, be aware of this strand in your own life as you read it.

Timing and pacing in learning

Some of the managers I have worked with are so used to working at a fast pace that they are extremely uncomfortable at the idea of spending even a day in a more reflective activity. Even on courses or development programmes they expect action, challenging case studies, embarrassing role-plays, punchy presentations. The transition from the pace of unreflective work to reflective learning they find extremely hard.

Cheryl I remember in particular. She was an extremely successful marketing manager in a pharmaceutical company, due for promotion. She had come on a five-day personal development programme because she realised that she had developed a challenging and abrasive style with her staff, which would not be appropriate in the job she was about to apply for. On the first day, where participants were expected to outline what they wanted from the programme, and what they would need from each other and the tutors to get it, she told us that she wanted to learn to listen better and appreciate the point of view of others. She realised, she said, that she needed to slow down a little. As the rest of the group described what they each wanted from the programme, Cheryl became more and more restless, in the end interrupting someone and saying "for Heaven's sake, can't we get on and do something" and then burst out laughing as she realised that she was doing the opposite of what she had said she wanted. With good humour she said "Well, you can see what I'm up against anyway," and relaxed a little. I felt very sympathetic as I too find a sudden change of pace and attention difficult to manage; but as Cheryl discovered by the end of the week, what can feel like pointless slowness can contain within it the same stimulating richness and interest that people can get from working at a high pace. It is a matter of adjusting the focus; taking time to reflect on long-term experiences or to debrief short-term development is an important feature of learning and developing. An addiction to action may be a way of avoiding learning from experience. Managing the rhythm and pacing of your learning from experience to include reflecting and "making sense of" is a necessary part of the process of development.

Learning through the job

A technique that I have found useful and have recommended in difficult and demanding work situations (although at first sight it seems rather silly), is to imagine that rather than this being a job it is a *course in doing this kind of job* – focusing on learning results as much as work results. This has two good effects – first, it helps me focus on what I am learning and, secondly, it gives me a different angle to working, helping me with delegation and with review. For example, if my job could be seen as "Diploma in Managing a Difficult Boss and Impossible Deadlines" – and that is what I am here to learn rather than anything which I can do easily – I am happy to delegate anything that does not contribute to my learning. It also helps me to review, because small steps count – "Am I getting better at managing a difficult boss – will I get an A grade or a B grade this month?"

When other people have used this approach it seems to help them focus their energy appropriately away from the frustrating activity of trying fruitlessly to change something that cannot be changed, into a more effective focus on "learning about" or "learning how to" where their energy is more usefully applied. It is also useful for people who are coping well with difficult work situations but feel dissatisfied. The "if this was a diploma in . . ." idea is amusing anyway, and the humour brings in a sense of ease. It also opens up the possibility of recognising and being pleased with what they are actually learning, as well as what they are achieving.

Managing your own development

There is an underlying philosophy to managing your own development. This philosophy includes the idea of taking responsibility for your own learning, whilst working with others to help you to learn and develop in the way that makes sense to you. It also involves the idea of "mapping" – that is, developing a picture of your present context, with some sense of what the future may bring. This map provides you with the possibilities of planning an appropriate route and destination for yourself. Effective mapping requires taking a wide view, being attentive to cues and clues that indicate what is and is not working for you now, and other cues that may give an early warning of what the future may bring. It also involves looking at the things that are not always looked at, as in the example above of "managing your boss". Sometimes the categories we are given in a curriculum or a book, or in the general social understanding that we have grown up with, do not match our own experience of what puzzles or delights us, and in what ways we want to develop. For this reason, we need to be fresh in our thinking as we map the landscape in which we are existing, and the path we want to take.

Looking back on your own life, you may notice that some of your greatest gains in knowledge, skills or understanding were taken on your own initiative, or were the result of learning from mistakes. The philosophy of "managing your own development" values and builds on this natural process.

8.1

This activity helps you to reflect on the kind of experiences that have been most useful to you in acquiring the skills, knowledge and experience that you currently have.

Step 1   *Take some time to review the course of your life so far. Identify the major phases and turning points.*

Step 2   *Which seem to have been the most enlightening? Which brought you to a new level of understanding or skill? Which were the most enjoyable?*

Step 3   *Can you draw any conclusions about how you might continue this development? Are there any experiences you might actively seek?*

Step 4   *Give yourself a moment to consider how you might learn more actively from what is happening to you now.*

Result   *This activity puts you in touch with the human developmental learning that you have naturally, and often unconsciously, been doing. It can provide an opportunity for you to do this more consciously and more proactively.*

Planning your own development

Explicitly or implicitly you need a plan or a purpose. You may prefer a structured, step-by-step approach to this, in which case Activity 8.2 may suit you. If you prefer to work more in terms of patterns and flows, you may prefer Activity 8.3.

activity

8.2

This activity helps you to draw up a realistic and workable development plan, of the kind that is often used at work, but is equally valuable at turning points in one's life. Use Table 8.1.

Table 8.1 Structure of a self-development plan

1. **Where I am now and how I got here**

   Current and expected work and role.
   Contribution, abilities and experience.
   Interests and what motivates me. Important factors in my life.
   Possible changes and what they will demand of me.
   Previous patterns of learning and development.
   The story of my life so far: experiences that have made me who I am.
   My values, and my purpose in life.

2. **Where or how I want to be, now or in the future**

   New skills, knowledge or experience that I need or want.
   Type of work I expect or plan to be doing.
   New situations I want to be able to respond to.
   How I want to develop my management or professional/technical skills.
   People that I want to influence or understand.
   How I want my life to be. Other areas of my life that are important, such as
      relationships, creative activity, philosophy/religion.

3. **What I will be doing to develop myself**

   What I will be learning, and how I will be learning it.
   Topics that I will be focusing on (up to six topics or areas).

   For each topic or area: experiences that will help me learn that topic:

      e.g. Projects I will take on
         People whom I will consult with or learn from
         Diaries I will keep for reflection etc.
         New behaviour or new strategies that I will try out
         Specific training that I will seek.

4. **Evidence of development**

   My criteria for success. How I will know that things are more the way I want
   them to be. What will be the difference?

   For each topic or area: The important observable difference when I have learned
   or developed in this area. What I will notice. What other people will notice. The
   main evidence that will show I achieved this learning or development goal.

   Overall, the evidence that I have moved forward in my self-development.

activity

8.3

*This activity is a way of planning for the present, rather than the
future. It can also help you prepare for unknown future experience.*

Step 1   *Using a "mind mapping" (Buzan, 1989) technique, map the different areas of your life, including for example present work, family and relationships, interests and passions, feelings about the present and future, attitude to or concerns about money. Diagrams 8.1 and 8.2 offer two examples.*

Step 2   *Notice any areas where you feel dissatisfied, blocked or anxious.*

Step 3   *Take one of the areas which could be improved, where you have some dissatisfaction. What would it take, on your part, to improve it? If you were better at something, such as communication, could you improve the situation? If you knew more, would that make a difference? Would improved understanding help? Do you need, at least, to learn not to waste energy on things which cannot be improved?*

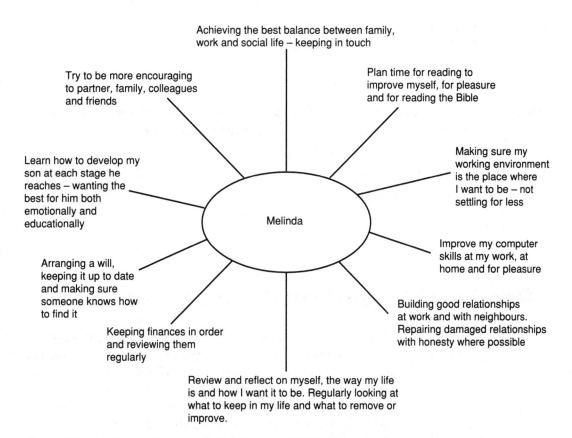

Figure 8.1   "Mind mapping" as a way of planning development. What do I want/what will I do? Melinda's map

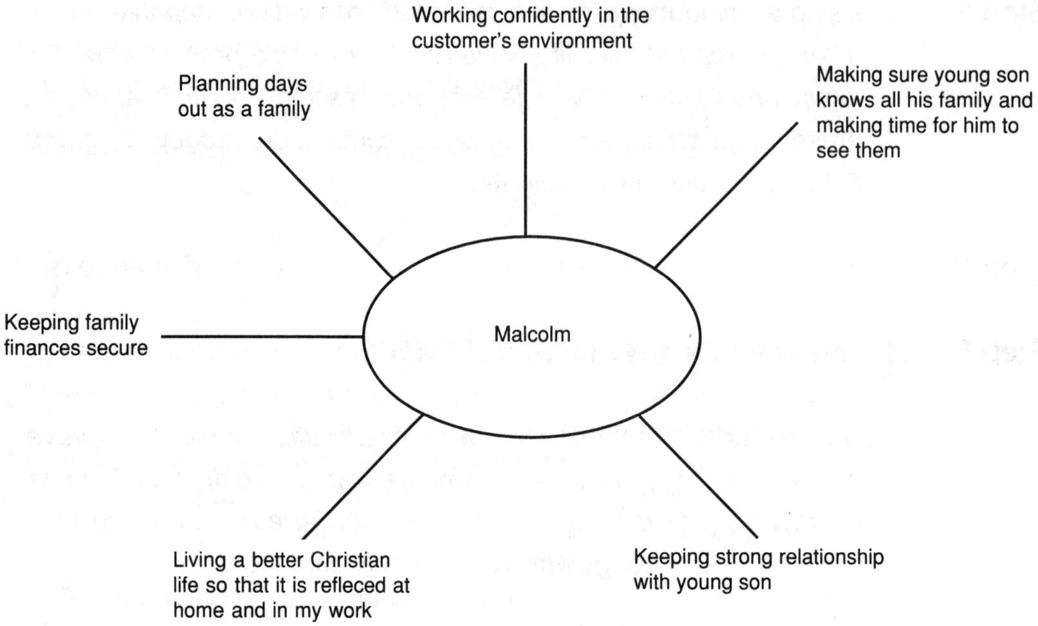

Figure 8.2 "Mind mapping" as a way of planning development. What do I want/what will I do? Malcolm's map

Step 4 *Write down one thing that you can do, practise or learn that could improve the situation. Write down when you will do it.*

Result *This activity puts you in a position to be able to highlight areas of your life where you can make a positive difference by improving your skills, knowledge or understanding.*

"Roads taken and roads not taken"

This is a useful concept in understanding the philosophy of managing your own development. We have all, during our lives, made choices which involved losing or giving up something in order to gain something else. Sometimes the things we gave up – ambitions, creative activity such as music, even sometimes our ideals – remain active, keep some meaning or importance for us throughout our lives. At certain turning points or critical moments, opportunities reappear to "follow the other road". If we are aware that the choices we left behind may still have energy for us, we are in a position to take the opportunities that arise. We may even want to be in readiness for the opportunity by remaining in a small way in touch with what the abandoned choice meant for us.

Getting support from others

One of the most useful things you can do for yourself is to get a mentor. Find someone who will listen while you talk through your situation, your needs and your plans. Even more useful is someone who will not only listen but also help you think things through in a way that stretches you. How to choose a mentor? Look for someone who is interested in you but not deeply involved: someone who can take a wider view, who can offer support when needed and challenge when needed. Arrange to meet them for an hour or so about five times a year.

The reflective practitioner

This concept was developed by Donald Schon in his book of the same title. It involves building in a reflective process as an intrinsic part of working, so that the experience of working automatically includes learning, improving and developing. It can also include building the ability to widen your outlook and a habit of looking for alternatives.

Sometimes our attitude to work, especially when under pressure, becomes more and more focused on the task in hand. When I get into this situation, I am reminded of a story:

At the bend of a deep and wide river, divers and doctors are gathered with a fleet of ambulances. They are pulling out and reviving scores of drowning people who are floating downstream. In spite of their heroic efforts, they could not save everyone. The leader is about to call for

DEVELOPING YOUR POTENTIAL

more doctors and ambulances. The most skilled doctor stops him, saying "let's go upstream and see who's pushing them in".

The reflective practitioner not only looks at their own work to develop to a level of excellence, but also sees the job in its context and reflects on its overall purpose. To be able to do this, we need "developmental working relationships" – people with whom we work, to whom we can talk about our work in a reflective way. We can develop a structure for this: a monthly meeting where each person in turn talks for half an hour about current work issues, with comments and reflections from their colleague as the model. I use in my own work two different colleagues. When I am working closely with another colleague for short periods of time, we take 20 minutes "debrief" every day with the question: "How are we doing?" The social work model of "non-managerial supervision" provides another structure. In a manufacturing setting, an effective quality circle provides yet another structure. The methods can be very different: the purpose is the same, that of finding a way to reflect on the way we work in order to improve. We may wish to improve effectiveness, or confidence, or job satisfaction, or level of skill. The reflective process can help in every case.

"Coaching questions"

The reflective process can in some cases be helped by a series of questions which you may ask yourself or get a colleague to ask you. Here are some examples of questions that help you to reflect on an incident that went well:

- What was satisfactory about the result?
- What do you think you did that helped?
- Was there anything about the circumstances that helped?
- How could you get this kind of result another time?
- Why was this result so satisfactory? What were you particularly pleased with? How come you are so satisfied?
- Were there any other results that were not so satisfactory? Was there also a downside?
- How has this incident taught you? Has it brought you to a new level of competence, or knowledge, or confidence? If so, how could you maintain that?

Conclusion

Taking an active part in understanding your own potential, and planning your own development can be very energising. It requires information and processes, and to some extent a systematic approach. Above all, it requires the ability and willingness to take some responsibility for your own development, and the common sense to get enlightened support from others.

9 You as part of the system

Introduction

● This chapter touches on the concepts of systems in a variety of ways: belief systems, global human systems, and systems thinking as a way of dealing with recurring issues. The theme is the importance, rather the necessity, of considering the wider system of which we are a part in a variety of ways. Working and thinking within our own narrow boundaries, without taking into account the nature of the system that we are part of, used to be possible and even effective. It is clear now, that it is not only ineffective but also dangerous. This is because the feedback loops are shorter and faster, as information flows are almost instantaneous. The effect of our actions in the system and the system's influence on us can take us by surprise. The set of interlinked reactions in Britain to the death of Diana Princess of Wales gives us an example of the various unpredictable flows of influence to and from groups of people. The complex reactions to and outcomes from Shell's attempt to dispose of the Brent Spar reminds us of the need also to look further into an unpredictable future than may have seemed necessary at the time it was built, for instance to be aware of issues of disposal. The apparent failure to do that left Shell in an impossible "no win" situation.

● Managing more with less is sometimes seen in a narrow way as getting other people to pay the price; so that someone else experiences the negatives of your actions. This book is advocating that what we need are the skills of working and managing in which we put our energy to its best use – physical, emotional and intellectual – in a sustainable and self-renewing way, that does not depend on externalising the results of our decisions or behaviour. There are many organisations where this is not easy to do. In these organisations the assumptions and belief systems are different, often based on an ethos of maximising short-term apparent gain without being held to account for waste and inefficiency that can be located outside the organisation – the principle of "externalising costs" – or located inside the organisation in terms of using people carelessly. The suggestions in this chapter – skills, techniques and ways of thinking – will help you work more effectively and humanly even in such an organisation. The benefit of a systems thinking approach is that it helps us to be aware of the systems at work that keep the organisation in such a state, and the links between the organisation and its context and the wider world.

Belief systems

The set of assumptions, the "taken-for-granted" beliefs I come across in my work with managers often surprise me. "Return to shareholders", "increasing market share" and other valid assumptions that belong quite properly in the limited language and truths of a business plan are extrapolated from where they properly belong and become values for living and working. The innate contradictions of these assumptions are never challenged (the ultimate goal of an ever "increasing market share" would obliterate the other icon "a free market", for example) and people are encouraged to see them as virtues rather than useful but limited conventions. I have worked with delightful managers who are good citizens and wise people who none the less slip into the trap, for example, of elevating "total commitment to the company" into the status of one of the ten commandments. I sometimes ask them to stop and think, take off the blinkers and reflect on what, in real life, merits total commitment. "A profit-driven company" does not come at the top of the list.

This is in no way to decry proper business values. A well-run business can bring creative employment, as well as prosperity and security. What we need to guard against is the extension of crude business principles into a philosophy for living. When we move into an organisation it is easy to be absorbed into a system of thinking and a set of values that are not necessarily our own, and may even clash with ours. Managing to exist within two sets of competing values uses energy, leaving us with stress and a feeling of fatigue, or with a spurious rather frantic energy which may lead us to do things within the organisation which we regret when we emerge from the "trance" of organisational life. How can we deal with this dilemma?

One strategy is to become informed about the basis of the assumptions underlying our work or our organisation. This means educating ourselves, so as to understand the real issues. This may involve reading the financial press, or joining organisations which provide information about the issues we need to grapple with such as corporate governance, business ethics, strategic thinking, current economic models. Some people deal with the dilemma by informing themselves about alternative views of the economic system (Hutton, 1996 Ormerod, 1995). For some people this wider and deeper knowledge can provide a sense of perspective and the ability to maintain their balance in the pressure of organisational life. Others challenge the assumptions by drawing attention to the "blatant discrepancies between common sense and economic rhetoric" (von Weisacker, Lovins and Lovins, 1997) and to the inconsistencies they see in the language of "competition" and "free markets". We need to learn to be accurate, knowing that in the current world system trade is distorted and, since prices do not represent the full costs of production (because of externalisation of costs), the market is not free in the first place. Prices and pricing systems in the "pseudo-market" that we operate in do not favour common sense, and sensible management of resources.

Another approach is to look more closely at the "theory" on which the economic rhetoric is based. Take, for example the often quoted value of competition and "survival of the fittest" as a basic natural law. This is supposedly based on the work of Darwin who, with others, developed the theory of evolution by natural selection. Darwin in his work observed the huge variety of species, and how they evolve to fill particular ecological niches. In his book *The Evolution of Species by Natural Selection* (Darwin, 1859), he was concerned to show how the constant interplay between variation and selection led to increased diversity and optimised use of the ecological base. This is not how the theory is used in the discourse and practice of economics, where the emphasis is on the potential of evolution to destroy small "varieties" and standardise products and markets.

We need as individuals to notice the way we manage ourselves in the system: noticing when we are being convinced by advertising, by peer or social pressure, or by "theories" to live and work in ways that are wasteful of our own resources, for short-term gains that in the end leave us depleted; depleted of energy, of affection, of a sense of real purpose.

Global systems

A further approach that helps us use our energy wisely is to gain a wider understanding of the whole system in which we are existing – the social system, the economic system, even the philosophical system – and to explore some of the interconnections between them. There are two routes into this. One is that of general education: reading, meeting people from different backgrounds, paying attention to current events and linking them into a wide framework of your own so that your experience inside the organisation is set into a wider interdependent context. This makes it possible to choose more wisely between actions you can take that will lead to change, and those that will only lead to frustration (although even actions "doomed to fail" they may still be worthwhile, if your motivation drives you that way, because in the long run, they can lead to increased awareness and change).

Systems thinking

A second route is to use a more direct systems-thinking approach, where you look more rigorously at the system and enquire about it in a structured way. Michael Balle (1994), in his book *Managing with Systems Thinking*, defines systems thinking as a way of focusing on relationships and patterns, rather than events and separate elements. It provides us with a different way of understanding what is going on, bringing a serious challenge to the logical but limited "only this causes only that" way of thinking to a more realistic "everything may affect everything else" approach, and also providing tools to help us find a way through the complexity. It can also alert us to the fact that our problems may be an inbuilt part of the system, sometimes even in the system that is designed to eliminate them. This way of thinking can also free us from the energy-consuming traps of blame and perceived helplessness.

9.1

This activity gives you the opportunity to try out a systems-thinking approach on a current situation that you find unsatisfactory, or which is taking a lot of your time and energy for little result.

Step 1 *Name and describe the situation you want to improve as specifically and succinctly as possible. Who is involved? What specifically is happening that disturbs you? What would you prefer to happen? Whose problem is it, actually?*

Step 2 *Review what you have written and clarify the assumptions you are making about the actual nature of the problem for you.*

Step 3 *What would be the criteria you would be monitoring to tell you that you were achieving your goal, or some resolution of the problem? What other conditions might also be relevant – or even more relevant, given the organisational purpose and goals?*

Step 4 *What resources are involved? Are they genuinely renewable, (and if so, at what scale) in the sense that if more is used on this situation, it does not mean using them up or taking them away from somewhere else.*

Step 5 *What actions are being taken? (By you or other people?) What information and assumptions is that action based on?*

Step 6 *What are the built in motivations? This means considering two aspects. We need to consider people's innate motivations (such as the wish for recognition and attention, for job satisfaction, for security of position, for some power over their own lives and some choice of action, for a sense of belonging etc.). We also need to consider the motivations that are built into the way the "system" or*

YOU AS PART OF THE SYSTEM

organisation is constructed. What are people rewarded for? What gets them attention? What leads to a rise in status, power, recognition? In both personal life and organisational life "we get what we reward", and this includes the formal and the informal reward system.

Result   *At this stage, you may already have given yourself enough information to take some significant action. You may find you are open to a different way of understanding the problem, based on the actual information you have been considering.*

I came across an example of this recently, from an educational psychologist, who had a recurrent problem with a boy, Billy, who hummed as he worked and was not at all communicative in school, although fairly sociable outside school. In particular, he did not speak to teachers. The educational psychologist was continually under pressure from teachers to treat Billy, and improve his classroom behaviour, and felt completely helpless because she had worked with him over three years and he had not changed. As she worked through the questions, these were some of the shifts she experienced.

The people involved were herself, the boy Billy, and the teachers he came into contact with. To begin with, she assumed that it was Billy's problem. On reviewing this, especially looking at the criteria and the organisational goals, she realised that he seemed to be happy and was learning, and his exam results were satisfactory. Who else was involved? Did he interfere with the learning of the other pupils? Apparently not. So the problem belonged to herself and the teachers, rather than to Billy. As she worked through the process, she began to be aware that the problem, for her, was that the teachers wanted her to take some action, to "cure" him. When she reviewed this further, it seemed that it was her reaction to their expectations of her that was the problem, especially as it used up her resources of time and energy both in listening to the teachers and working with the boy.

She began to review her actions, and her own motivation which came through not only as a commitment to help pupils, but also a need to be respected as a competent professional by teachers, and give them what they wanted. This brought her suddenly to the moment when she decided to run workshops for the teachers on the topic of appropriate responses to unconventional classroom behaviour, including Billy's humming. This would be a more appropriate way of using her energy and time, would shift the repetitive pattern that she and the teachers had been in, and would take all of them forward to a new level of competence and understanding. It honoured their various motivations, and in a more creative way than their previous pattern had done.

Another aspect of systems thinking that can be applied in our everyday lives is that of learning more about the relationship we (or our team or our organisation or family) are creating with its environment, and how that dynamic equilibrium or dance is being maintained. What feedback or information are you giving and getting? What effect is it having? Reflecting on this can give you some insights into where feedback or information is having a large or small effect on you and how you are responding. You may find that some kinds of feedback are triggering an exaggerated response in you: criticism for instance, or threats of losing money. How is your reaction affecting the people around you (your environment), and how in turn do you respond to that reaction? There may be a different way for this reaction to happen that would take you nearer to your goals, or take up less of your energy.

Freedom and regulation

Systems thinking gives us other useful tactics or concepts for managing in complex and long-term situations. The "tragedy of the commons" is a story which illuminates the need for balance between freedom and regulation in the management of resources.

This familiar example tells of the experience of managing the "common pasture" in medieval Britain. A common pasture is available for all to graze their cows freely, and is a necessary resource for the village. It is destroyed when an individual decides to increase his herd, as the pasture is plentiful and free, in order to grow rich. Others follow suit. The common becomes overgrazed, the cows gradually starve, and so may the village.

This is a stark example of a system we see throughout the world: using a freely available resource on the basis of individual need and profit leads first to profit for individuals. The sum of those actions leads, however, to disaster for the individuals. In modern life we see, for example, depletion of fish stocks in the North Sea, and overgrazing in the Sahel.

In organisational life I have seen an example where using the competitive principle to increase departmental performance decreases overall performance. In a marketing department brand managers competed against each other for rewards and bonuses, based on increasing targets. To begin with, this had an excellent effect on overall performance: everyone was selling more in order to beat their colleagues. This habit and style worked against them, however, when the external market-place became tougher. Because of the internal competition, they would never support another manager's brand or cross-sell, because if someone else got more, they got less. The overall performance declined, until the reward system was changed so that elements of cooperation for the common good were recognised in the reward and recognition system.

This example and many others remind us that a system that works well in one set of circumstances may be disastrous when the circumstances change. A way of thinking, such as systems thinking, that helps us to be aware of shifts in the external system, and the longer-term effects of a solution that works in the short term, is essential if we are to manage more change and complexity with less losses and disasters.

"Fit", "split", and the need for variety

"Fit" and "split" are used by Richard Pascale as ways of describing the need for balance between a set of guiding principles and values, which do not however become too unreflective, cosy or ossified, and a method for engaging with conflict as a transformational force for new ideas and ways of moving on. This is suggested for organisations, and it is also useful in individual life. As I have through life become aware of my own core values, it has also seemed essential to test them and refresh them in new and challenging situations, where they sometimes come out differently or are transformed. To survive in a difficult organisation, especially one where the values do not match your own, it is a vital process.

activity

9.2

This activity gives you the opportunity to reflect on how your system of values matches or challenges the values of the organisation or informal system in which you work, and to find a way of understanding and perhaps reconciling the two sets of values. This can have a clarifying and relaxing effect: even if the values are different, it is easier to cope when you are clear about the differences, than when you are unclear and vaguely dissatisfied.

Step 1   *Write down six choices you have recently made, some comparatively major and some fairly minor.*

Step 2   *For each choice, imagine an outsider was observing the way you chose. What might they deduce about your values and priorities?*

Step 3   *Use the "five why" technique. For one of the choices, write down why you made the choice; then ask why again, about the reason for the choice, and continue the process until you have asked why five times. In many cases this brings you quickly to some core values.*

Step 4   *Use the "categorical imperative" to test some of your choices: if everyone made the same choice as you, what would be the result?*

Step 5   *Use the same approaches to explore some choices recently made by "the organisation" that you work in, again with a mixture of major and minor decisions.*

Result   *This will begin to give you a picture of the match or mismatch between your value system and that of the organisation. You may also find that you want to think more deeply about clarifying your own values and understanding the processes inside the organisation and the people involved.*

Conclusion

In this chapter we have looked at the wider systems of which we are a part, paying particular attention to the belief systems and assumptions by which we and others operate, and seeing where there may be discrepancies that we should challenge. We have also reviewed the systems-thinking approach as a way both of understanding the system, and dealing with problems.

10 In conclusion

In the previous chapters, the theme has been ways of managing our work and our lives that are effective and efficient, that make sense and that match our values. I have approached the topic from many perspectives, to provide choice and a three-dimensional approach. The trigger for my thinking has always been a situation that does not seem to make sense. I have noticed where I or other people have unwittingly been using time and energy in ways that are unproductive in the human sense and that do not lead to real gain, extrinsic or intrinsic, and may even, when we stop to look at it, be leading to serious loss. This has generally seemed to happen when we are in the grip of un-thought-through assumptions and fears or are trying to work to mismatched goals. What seems to be necessary is a light touch, an ability to detect inconsistencies and a willingness to change in ways that make a difference.

Bibliography

Adair, J. (1988). *Effective Decision Making*. Pan Books.

Balle, M. (1994). *Managing with Systems Thinking*. McGraw-Hill.

Beck, A. (1987). *Rational Thinking*. Psychology Today.

de Bono, E. (1985). *Six Thinking Hats*. Little Brown.

Burgel, K. and Burgel, A. (ed.) (1997). *Memories of Childhood and Youth, Albert Schweitzer*. Syracuse.

Butler, G. and Hope, T. (1997). *Manage Your Mind*. Oxford University Press.

Buzan, T. (1989). *Use Both Sides of Your Brain*. Plume.

Caproni, P. J. (1997). *Applied Behavioural Science*, **33**(1).

Covey, S. R. (1992). *The Seven Habits of Highly Effective People*. Simon and Schuster.

Darwin, C. (1859). *The Evolution of Species by Natural Selection*.

Dryden, W. (1989). *Rational Emotive Counselling in Action*. Sage.

Ellis, A. (1994). *Theory and Practice of Rational Emotive Therapy*. Souvenir Press.

Fisher R. and Ury, W. (1997). *Getting to Yes*. Arrow Books.

Gilbert, G. N. and Mulkay, M. (1984). *Opening Pandora's Box*. Cambridge University Press.

Goldratt, E. M. and Cox, J. (1995). *The Goal*. Gower.

Goldsmith, M. and Wharton, M. (1993) *Knowing Me, Knowing You, Exploring Personality Type and Temperament*. SPCK.

Goleman, D. (1996). *Emotional Intelligence*. Bloomsbury.

Gray, J. (1993). *Men are from Mars, Women are from Venus*. Thorsons.

Heirs, B. J. (1987). *The Professional Decision-Thinker*. Dodd Mead.

Hill, L. and Kamprath, N. (1991). *Beyond the Myth of the Perfect Mentor: Building a Network of Developmental Relationships*. Harvard Business School.

Honey, P. (1997). *Chairing Meetings*. Peter Honey.

Hutton, W. (1996). *The State We're In*. Vintage.

Kiersey, D. and Bates, M. (1984). *Please Understand Me*. Gnosology Books.

Mole, J. (1995). *Mind your Manners*. Nicholas Brealey.

Myers, I. (1962). *Manual: The Myers Briggs Type Indicator*. Consulting Psychologists Press.

Pascale, R. (1991). *Managing on the Edge*. Penguin.

Ogilvy, J. (1995). *Living without a Goal. Finding the Freedom to Live a Creative and Innovative Life*. Doubleday.

Ormerod, P. (1995). *The Death of Economics*. Faber.

Reynolds, D. K. (1984). *Playing Ball on Running Water*. Quill.

Rhodes, J. (1991). *Conceptual Toolmaking*. Basil Blackwell.

Rosenberg, M. (1996). Interviewed in the *Monthly Aspectarian*.

Salmon, P. (1985). *Living in Time*. J. M. Denton & Sons.

Schon, D. (1995). *The Reflective Practitioner: How Professionals Think in Action*. Arena.

Seligman, M. (1992). *Learned Optimism*. Pocket Books.

Stacey, R. (1992). *Managing Chaos*. Kogan Page.

Tannen, D. (1991). *You Just Don't Understand: Women and Men Talking Together*. Virago Press.

Trompenaars, F. (1993). *Riding the Waves of Culture*. The Economist Books.

Ury, W. (1992). *Getting Past No*. Century Business.

Watts, A. (1992). *The Wisdom of Insecurity*. Rider Books.

Wilson, P. (1995). *The Calm Technique*. Thorsons.

von Weisacker, E., Lovins, A. B. and Lovins, L. H. (1997). *Factor Four: Doubling Wealth, Halving Resource Use*. Earthscan.

Index